MY SECRET GARDEN SHED

. . . is a collection of men's sexual fantasies and confessions of all kinds, from the sensual to the downright bizarre, and from the sublime to the downright pervy. Dispatches from the depths of the male psyche, they have been solicited through advertisements placed in magazines, both mainstream and adult, and on the internet, presenting a unique cross-section of men's sexual tastes.

Paul Scott is an editor of erotic fiction

MY SECRET GARDEN SHED

True-Life Male Sexual Fantasies

Compiled and Edited
by Paul Scott

*Thanks to CN at PI, CD at Moondance Media
and GS at Fantasy*

*This book is dedicated to everyone who
has contributed to it.
However small your deposit, thank you.*

This book is a work of fantasy.
In real life, make sure you practise safe, sane and
consensual sex.

First published in 2002 by
Nexus
Thames Wharf Studios
Rainville Road
London W6 9HA

www.nexus-books.co.uk

Typeset by TW Typesetting, Plymouth, Devon
Printed and bound by Clays Ltd, St Ives PLC

ISBN 0 352 33725 7

Contents

Introduction

Snips, snails and puppy dogs' tails

Firstly there's one thing I should get straight. This book is not a work of sexual politics. It's a collection of male masturbation fantasies. If it contains any sociological insights, or offers a contribution to any ongoing debate, then it does so by accident. It's not a clarion call for anyone's nascent men's movement. It's neither an exhortation to grow beards, take to the woods and beat drums, nor to flutter our eyelashes and learn how best to be office totty for the sake of career advancement. Men, it *won't* tell you how to juggle your work/life balance, improve your sex life, or become more self-empowered.

Though gender difference and sexual orientation is something that divides us in the sexual sphere, it is not absolute. First and foremost, as men and women we're individuals, each of us with our own unique perspective on the conflicts and contradictions of life. As anyone who has spent time knocking around with politically active students will know, wearing badges divides as much as it unites. The most worthy cause can engender the most Machiavellian internal wranglings. By contrast, that which seems beyond the pale can sometimes demonstrate a heartening virtue. A badge is no guarantee of consensus, it merely signifies the assumption of one, and there's both good and

1

bad in any self-styled grouping which invites us to ally ourselves with it, and good and bad in all of us, too.

For example, a growing number of western men are saying that in some ways – fairly small ones in the scheme of these things – it's a tough time to be a man. Take for example our representation in the media – and how we're viewed in the society it reflects. For starters, there's the staple 'stupid man' of European and American advertising. Invariably slightly over-weight, he's the guy who trudges to the bank in the rain to find out it's closed, while his smart and sylphlike partner finds that miracle loan they need, effortlessly, on the internet. (She's inexplicably at-tached to him in some codependent hell, for she'd clearly do far better elsewhere.) Then there's the soap-opera villain, who returns time and again to stalk, murder and menace his co-stars with an improbable frequency driven by a TV ratings war. While on the subject of demonisation, a single man living alone is often seen as sad, weird, or even as the local loner, suspect. A woman in the same situation is independent, feisty. In much the same way, female masturbation is a mark of self-sufficiency, a prime-time staple on *Sex in the City*, while you can still insult a man by calling him a wanker.

A small percentage of men have the luck to earn 'fat cat' salaries, retire at fifty to a non-executive stipendiary and take two holidays a year. Glass ceilings or not, because the people who inhabit this world of helicopters and Lexuses are almost exclus-ively male, the opportunities are often perceived to be there for all men, regardless of the small number of such roles which exist in reality. And as men we too have our own glass ceilings, and we've perfected discrimination against each other as much if not more than we have against women. Meanwhile, our potential as carers is frequently overlooked by careers advisers and child-custody courts alike. And there's a growing number of working women who'd agree that the benefits of feminism's hard-won economic agency are to be weighed and balanced by anyone who bears the responsibilities that come with it, and juggles financial arrears against assets on a regular basis – in the face of the consistent necessity of consumption that typifies life for both sexes in the First World.

In most of the western world, working women have yet to achieve absolute parity of income with their male counterparts, and negative perceptions persist regarding a woman's propensity to 'drop out' of the workplace and have children (which operates to the detriment of their male partners too). Nonetheless, it's hard to feel sympathy for a broker or city fund manager, on a basic salary at least four times the national average, who has successfully sued for sexual discrimination because her obscenely high Christmas bonus was less than that of male colleagues. The gender issue here obscures the fact, meanwhile, that the City of London couldn't give a hoot about the British public. We've been mis-sold endowments, shares are worth less than they were, and our pensions won't keep us. Although the success of such a suit is justified on its own terms, where is the wider context of social justice, for the benefit of all?

For much of human history women were seen as goods and chattels, as they continue to be in a frightening number of places – especially in the Middle East and North Africa. It wasn't uncommon in English rural life as late as the late eighteenth century, for example, to hear of a wife sale, in which a man would auction his wife in public, often on a market day, before an assembled throng. In reality, by this point, the 'sale' was stage-managed with the wife's consent, and the successful bidder a man with whom she had begun an affair. It was seen by the husband as a way of ceding his wife to a man whose emotional claim was now perhaps greater than his own, with some dignity. Nonetheless, the symbolism of personal ownership and contractual exchange remained, along with the humiliating public context, from the then-recent days of the branks and the ducking stool. Back in the day, we learn, when women were financially dependent on men and the only other options were the street or the workhouse, it was the lucky wife whose husband did not stagger home with the remnants of the housekeeping from the pub.

But beware the clichés: for every wife-beating good-for-nothing in a porter-stained vest, there were nine men like my grandfather, who, having fought for his country, wanted nothing more than to settle into the social fabric, to carry on making sacrifices; who took from the women in his life no more than he gave back, and relaxed with a light ale from time to time. For all the media tells us about absentee fathers, football hooligans, gang culture; for all it presents men as stubbly, lupine villains and irresponsible sexual predators – or else as inane comic relief – it's worth remembering that most of us set out to lead sober (well, in the broadest sense), socially responsible lives. A majority of men, I'd contend, aim to live much as my grandfather did, or its cultural equivalent, and perhaps therefore we deserve to be portrayed a little better than we are in the above examples. Even though as a gender we're capable of acts of unbelievable evil, from the contributions I received in answer to the survey detailed in the next chapter, I'd say – partly to my own surprise – that although I was touring the fetid byways of hidden male sexuality, the replies I got were generally from the former more thoughtful, and often misrepresented, – *ahem* – rump of the male population.

But let's put away the violins, and not get precious. When it comes to the 'sexist' representation of men as objects of desire, on television and in magazines and advertising, who cares? In the mid-90s, a cosmetics company ran a poster ad campaign in the UK which showed a woman's stiletto heel inserted between the ass-cheeks of a naked, anonymous, but evidently gorgeous, man. I recall there was some male opprobrium in the letters pages of the broadsheet papers, along the lines of 'now women can be more sexist than we can', or similar sour grapes – grown in a glass house. I also recall that any man with a genuine understanding of fetishism couldn't have cared less. Because they grasped that, in a playful, sexual context, the more you can take then the more you're entitled to dish out. I'd say to men who feel as those respondents did: live a little, be objectified, allow yourself to be 'humiliated'. You might be surprised by the trust – and the sexual licence – you get back.

On a similar note, one mild-mannered survey respondent complained that *Sex and the City* objectifies men, and it's been said that this represents a trend on the part of programme-makers. I don't think it's naïve not to find this a problem if the context is sexual. After all, some of us quite like it! Conversely, if you're the fast-lane-hoggin' Madonna-whore-con-fusin' woman-hatin' date-rapin' archetypal spoilt little boy who can't tell the difference between fantasy and reality – and can't keep his hands to himself – then you'd better watch out for the righteous kick in the balls you're patently cruising for.

* * *

In 1979, Nancy Friday published *My Secret Garden*, a collection of women's sexual fantasies which has gone on to become a benchmark text of sexual politics *and* women's erotica. On publication, the surrealism, depravity and extremity of many of the fantasies – a cornucopia in which horses have star turns – took pundits by surprise. And the book deserved the attention it garnered because it made a timely point in an accessible way, one that must have been, and still is, reassuring to many: that there's a difference between a fantasy and desire. What we think we want in fantasy we don't necessarily wish to act out in real life.

Sexual fantasy is a private, no-holds-barred dojo in which we wrestle with the unexplored, safe from self-judgement and the judgement of our peers, whereas we're inclined to desire the known, or the nearly-known. We may believe we really want it while we're indulging in our created sexual world, for the fantasy to work, but in our mind we can be completely elsewhere to the physical reality, and may always remain so. Let's face it, you wouldn't *really* want to see that submissive execution fantasy through to the bitter end. Concomitantly, keeping that sex-slave full-time would be quite a commitment – they're not just for Christmas. So be at ease with yourself, whoever that may be. Examine your fantasies for what they represent, don't sweat them. They're only the prognosis for your future behaviour that you choose to make them. Black Lace published their *Book of Women's Sexual Fantasies* in 1999, making the argument by extension that embracing female submission did not entail rejecting a feminist lifestyle, and it was literal-minded to think it did. On the contrary, as the cliché has it, many subs are seeking relief from the responsibility they're ordinarily called on to exercise. None of this is to say, of course, that we don't most of the time have fantasies we'd be more than perfectly happy to see become reality!

I approached the business of compiling this book with something of a cynical approach, expecting to look under stones and turn up all manner of unsavoury impulses. To poke with a stick into the mud at the bottom of the pool until the water clouded with the stench-ridden mulch of long-repressed, fetid fantasies. I thought I'd be in for the prose equivalent of a few used man-size tissues that plopped in through the post, at least. In truth, I was slightly ashamed of this attitude once I'd sifted enough responses to the advertisements (the ones soliciting sexual fantasies that I'd placed in publications and which are detailed in the following chapter) to find that they were almost one hundred per cent from chaps who registered their interest in good faith, wanted to know more about the nature and direction of the project, whether the editorial angle was sympathetic or whether I was going to present their most intimate thoughts as entertainment, a freak-show stitch-up. In the cases where the dialogue went that far, I told them it would be something of both. And I received some of the fullest responses from people who'd approached me consideredly and gingerly in the first place. I soon dropped my condescension as I realised that the respondents were making a leap of faith, and more so than me. Depraved and corrupted though I may be by my few years of editing fetish fiction, compiling this book was heartwarming in the open expression of trust and human idiosyncrasy it yielded. I found out that, at least among the men who are going to bite at an ad such as mine, there's a lot of sexual self-determination. I'd like to extend, while I have the chance to, my heartfelt thanks to everyone who contributed. Almost without exception, you answered a sincere inquiry with a sincere response. Much appreciated.

* * *

Socially, we've once again come full semicircle, if you like, from the late 80s, when the male sexual repression was not uncommonly seen in any expression of male sexual desire. It's a question of context, and a reflection of the growth of women's freedom to express themselves sexually, which perhaps encourages a greater understanding of men doing the same, now they no longer have sole rights to such self-expression. Certainly, if done with self-awareness and pastiche (and not apologism), it seems more acceptable for men to have a gander at one of the many burgeoning pole-dancing establishments in the UK and the USA, for example. Concomitantly, one hopes, women are able to think of outrageous slut behaviour as a lifestyle choice these days! That's to an extent true in my liberal north London ghetto, still maybe not so in a provincial backstreet. Whatever, the balance is to be at ease with yourself while being self-controlled.

Another byproduct of women's sexual empowerment has been a tendency for women not to *presume* that they understand male sexuality (I hope I'm returning the favour despite my generalisations), even where we're unimpressively predictable animals from time to time, slobbed out, burping, in front of the football. The last few years has seen a growth – largely amongst a female book-buying market – of so-called lad-lit (more accurately bloke-lit), or dad-lit, such as is found in the writing of Nick Hornby or Tony Parsons; books which purport to detail the male psyche in what is to some extent a generally representative way. Then there are the more obviously female-pitched offerings of Mike Gayle, whose *Mr Commitment* provides a wish-fulfilment ending for the Bridget Jones generation, and Mark Mason's *What Men Think About Sex*, with its expository title that leaves you in no doubt as to its intended market. In the meantime, chic-lit has also grown as a literary trend, from the early and unexpected success of Bridget Jones. Compared even to the humour of Helen Fielding's *Independent* column, and that of the two Bridget Jones books, you'd perhaps be forgiven for thinking that some of her successors have tapped in to a feisty-female formula, with male characters who are bland, whether chisel-jawed Lotharios or hapless post-Lucky Jims, without exception. (OK, OK, I know – erotic fiction; glass houses and stones again come to mind. Don't you know that novels such as *The Mistress of Payne Hall* and *Bond-Slave of the Orinoco* have almost Hamlet-like levels of motivation and self-analysis?)

The amount of popular culture aimed at women grows the more spending power women acquire, of course. The female car-buying market is the best thing that's happened to car commercials in years, for example, banishing endless footage of squealing tyres on California's coastal highway, and reflecting a world in which 'one lady owner' no longer carries weight as a recommendation in a used car ad. As women increase their spending on drama, fiction and film, it becomes worth asking how representative the images of male sexuality therein remain. (But men – there's no monstrous regiment of feminist fascism sweeping over the horizon towards us. We do it to each other – look who sits around boardroom tables.) A desire to find out who we are these days was one reason for this book. Contrary to popular belief, I'd contend that a majority of men don't regularly swap notes about sex with each other, beyond conversations of a 'look at the *xyz* on that' variety, and anecdotes about *how* they got a partner into bed, rather than what they did when they got there. To do so, to a lot of self-consciously hetero men, remains kind of – well – *gay*. As psychiatrist William Godley, who has studied the way American men interact with each other, says: 'Women are far more comfortable with talking about the intimate details of their lives, including sex. I would even go as far as to say that it is the requisite of a close female friend that they are expected to spill the beans to some extent. A group of male friends might discuss their relationship or how things are for them sexually, but in a far less revelatory way. This greater need for privacy makes men feel uncomfortable with the kind of female discussion you see on *Sex and the City*. It is perceived as gross disloyalty. They would absolutely hate the women they are involved with to speak about them like that.'

Why *My Secret Garden Shed*? Because the book will follow the point of view that we should be at ease with our fantasies, because not every fantasy is one we'd necessarily like to have *really* happen. And imagine a grandfatherly shed, traditionally with its arcane, rusted, cobwebbed garden tools; its sievelike thing, the use of which always remained a mystery; its jars full of nails etc, fastened by their lids to the underside of the shelf above, a smell of creosote. At the bottom, half-observed with some surprise, would be a small box of porn mags from the soft-focus 70s, their covers crinkled with damp. There, next to the old chair with its beaten-up cushion and his roll-up paraphernalia and grandfatherly bottle of light ale. Or else on the wooden walls would be forgotten bombshells – faded, drawing-pinned postcards from another era. The fantasies in this book are as diverse as they are perverse, revealing hidden and original gems from the private byways of maleness. Contrary to the slippery images of feminine beauty held up for us by Hollywood, you might be surprised at some of the curious places and people in which the respondents here find arousal, and also perhaps by the everydayness of some. Forget about the *haute couture* numbers that starlets wear to premieres, it seems. Think instead of his mum's old mac, of the dullest but unintentionally tightest catalogue clothes, of a uniform, a business suit, of Bridget Jones' big knickers, until the sensuality to be found in everyday life itself too becomes a fetish, along with all the others, and we can all relax.

1

The Survey

Who, Why, Where, When and What
From LA to Eastern Germany, and including Japan,
the developed world supports a *huge* porn industry,
aimed predominantly at men. Since the strictures on
selling hardcore pornography were relaxed in the UK
in September 2000, the British Board of Film Classifi-
cation has passed over 250 hardcore video titles for
sale uncut in licensed sex shops. In the USA, just about
every city sports a 'Porn Barn'-style outlet on the edge
of town, selling mags, videos and DVDs as high-
volume products. In a nation of such cultural diver-
sity, which encompasses both those who sleep, eat and
live an SM lifestyle, and those, of the Christian Right
for example, who find the commercialisation of sex
offensive, a look at the producers of pornography will
reveal a number of blue-chip corporate names – even if
their pornographic output is branded so as to keep the
product at arm's length from the parent media group's
more familiar offerings in book and music stores and
movie theatres throughout the nation.

So how true are the porn clichés? It's hard to assess
how much market research is undertaken by the

pornography industry. One LA-based film director and studio partner I spoke to told me that his studio basically took a suck-it-and-see approach, as it were, to the content and packaging of hardcore films (by which I'll simply mean films that show penetration of anywhere but the mouth, and by an erect penis). In other words, they picked up on what the competition did and copied that, or pastiched the approach of previous pornographers, from the corn-fed, freckled pleasures of *Debbie Does Dallas*, to dark, gothic fantasy. The product is its own market research. If so, they might find this book useful, as it attempts to offer something of an answer to the question of what men want as fantasy, while accepting, of course, that there are as many different answers as there are men in the world.

To solicit the responses I needed for this book, I placed ads in various publications, and trawled the Net for opinion. There were broadly two ads used, excepting minor changes to make the wording specific as required: one appealing to people who were probably familiar with the idea, at least, of correspondence about sex as undertaken in chatrooms and the fetish and swinging 'communities', intended for adult and fetish magazines; the other aimed at readers of mainstream magazines, where a little more persuasion might be required. I was wrong. There were just as many responses, for example, from *Private Eye* as there were from *Desire*, with approximately the same size box ad placed in each. The difference was that the correspondents from the former would have more questions about the nature of the project, engage in a bit of debate, and do it all name and address supplied. The correspondents who replied to *Desire* were more familiar with the notion of hitting a total stranger from the outset with the innermost details of their sexuality and, *quid pro quo*, a lot who did replied so anonymously. I'm pleased to say I received nothing, however, which gave rise to the moral dilemma of whether or not I should responsibly pass it to the police.

The two styles of ad are reprinted here:

MEN – RESPONSIBLE, APPROACHABLE, UNSHOCKABLE MASS-MARKET PUBLISHER WOUD LIKE TO HEAR YOUR SEXUAL FANTASIES, FOR A FORTHCOMING BOOK PROJECT – from the sensual to the downright bizarre. Write anonymously if you wish but if you include a return address we will include an erotic novel, stocks permitting. Reply in confidence to . . . Personal information will not be kept beyond the length of correspondence, added to any database or shared commercially in any way.

MEN – MAINSTREAM UK PUBLISHER WANTS TO HEAR YOUR SEXUAL FANTASIES: from the filthy to the downright bizarre. Pervs dom and sub, bis, TVs most welcome, no holds barred. Write anonymously if you wish but if you include a return address we will send you a free erotic novel, stocks permitting.

Where it was appropriate, in other words where the respondent requested more information from me about the project and hadn't leaped on the chance to submit to me their filthiest sexual fantasy, I returned a questionnaire along the following lines, designed to find out a little background on them, and to tease out their sexual thoughts further. If this sounds transparently prurient, like a hardcore Henry Mayhew with-

14

out the talent or time, then that's because I *am* transparently prurient. To this end, the survey is reprinted at the back of this book too, and if you wish to be included in a similar collection to this, then fill it in and send it to the freepost (UK only) address given (or you can email me at *paulscott01uk@ yahoo.co.uk*).

Nexus

Male Sexual Fantasy in the 21st Century

A. QUESTIONS ABOUT YOU
1. What is your age? . . . years
2. Are you single . . . or in a long-term partnership or marriage . . .?
3. Are you: heterosexual . . . homosexual . . . or bisexual . . .?

What, if anything, do you find offensive? Please list things – objects, actions or even attitudes – which are to do with sex or which are often associated with sex and which offend you.

4. in photographs, on television or in films
5. in novels
6. in real life

B. ABOUT YOUR SEXUAL FANTASIES (Definition: What you think about when you think about sex in such a way that you become sexually aroused.)

1. How often, on average, do you have sexual fantasies: several times a day? . . . Once a day?

... A few times a week? ... A few times a
month? ... Hardly ever? ...
2. Do your fantasies tend to have recurring themes
or subjects? ... Or is each fantasy very different?
...
3. If there are recurring themes or subjects, what
are they?
4. Do you have a current favourite fantasy, or a
fantasy that you enjoy more than most?

C. ABOUT YOUR SEXUALITY
1. Think back to when you were discovering your
sexuality, your sexual orientation, and the sexual themes that are now part of your personality. What did you find erotic in those days?
What things (for instance films, or books, or
items of clothing) or people or experiences were
a turn-on?
2. What things or people or experiences are particular turn-ons now?
3. Describe the best sex you've ever had (so far!).
As before, continue on a separate sheet if you
prefer.
4. What would improve your sex life?

* * *

The actual fantasies I received ranged from those
which were presented in story form, to those presented in the baldest blow-by-blow narrative. They
ranged from the most structured, erudite third-person
narratives to random mind-wanderings and half-
articulated lust. Then there are those which are
simply confessional, as if told by someone in a pub
or bar. In the cause of entertainment, I've unscientifi-
cally but nonetheless appropriately included some of

the gems of the choice, unsolicited post we've received at Nexus here and there.

I've also included a few of my own fantasies. Although, of course, I have to differing degrees edited and rewritten all of the following ones, so they'll all be of a style despite their differing content, I think in each case they've remained true to the senders' intent. If you think you've spotted one that's mine, why not email me and see if your hunch is correct?

There's little herein that's man-on-man, simply because, given the plurality and evolvedness of gay culture, that's a whole book(s) in itself. A project has to have set limits if you're ever going to finish it, so this ad didn't appear in specifically gay publications. Where gay action appears in the fantasies, it's within the envelope of transvestism (which as presented here is an invariably straight activity but which can involve bi-curious activity, often to the end of submission or humiliation), transsexuals as fantasy figures, and the sort of enforced behaviour which to an extent obviates the need for a man who finds it important to think of himself as straight to face his sexual confusion. It also deals with curiosity about such things as having one's prostate tickled, or what it's like to give a blow job, as felt by men who don't necessarily find they want to turn their heads to look at other men passing by in the street. Broadly, it includes the ways in which such boundaries have been crossed on the fetish scene, in which the phenomenon of mixed clubs prefigured their appearance in dance culture by a good few years. It's a phenomenon which is good to see if you ultimately find labels divisive. Personally, I don't find it a cop-out to think of human beings as essentially neither hetero or homo – just *sexual*.

I divided the responses I received into categories much along the lines of how advertisers in a contact magazine would choose to define their sexuality, but also according to certain distinctions within those envelopes for which I'll explain the rationale. The responses from men who expressed a dominant side to their sexuality I divided into those who emphasised the thrill to be gained from humiliating or embarrassing their imaginary partner (in a self-aware, sexualised context – not just by farting loudly in company, for example) and those who expressed a specific interest in corporal punishment or discipline. (In other words, those whose ideal partner, on the basis of this survey, would be a sexual submissive, and those whose ideal partner would be masochistic.) Interestingly, among men who identified themselves as submissive, no such distinction could be made, since all the responses without exception blurred the line between the two. For the purposes of definition, sexual submission does not necessarily involve pain. A person can be a submissive and still hate pain. A masochist who enjoys pain may or may not be a submissive, but invariably is. The largest number of respondents, not surprisingly perhaps, fell into the group which was not especially interested in the compelling power of sub/dom games and SM, but whose sexuality goes at least to some degree beyond vanilla sex (i.e. good old missionary activity, or any of the gamut of positions you'll find in sex manuals, which remain for all but the most lifestyle pervs the most meaningful sex most people have) to involve some form of 'perversion' or fetishistic interest. I've called these people the playful pervs. The results are as follows:

Vanilla sex exclusively	13.32%
Playful Pervs	33.3%
(mess and fetish)	

Male submissive	13.32%
Male dom – SM/CP (pain)	17.76%
Male dom – power games	11.1%
(some restraint but no pain)	
X-dressing	4.44%

The proportion of responses that were too taboo (in other words they would require a whole book in themselves, and a different one to this – about the nature of taste; and how much taboos have any rational basis, by coinciding with activities which are actually harmful. It would be a far weightier tome than this.) came out at 6.76 per cent.

These apart, the following were areas I thought it of interest to have a figure on:

- Of the fantasies which were kinky to any degree (i.e. a figure of around 86% of the total, that's excluding group sex and gay activity as kinky in themselves);
- 27.9% involved some form of restraint,
- 23.26% involved corporal punishment (with either hand or any of the accepted instruments of discipline – cane, crop, paddle, tawse and any I've forgotten. Among the less realistic, whips, cats,
- Only 5.17% of kinky fantasies involved both – that's less of an intersection, if presented as a Venn diagram, than you might expect,
- 11.1% of all fantasies involved semi-public display, whether as a part of group sex or exhibitionism, or as a part of SM ritual,
- 98% of respondents described themselves as straight, but 17.78% had sexual thoughts about other men

It's interesting to see the number of bi-curious fantasies (excluding the lipstick lesbians of porn cliché!) as a percentage of the total, whether kinky or not, and it would also be interesting to establish the ratio between fantasies which feature real women – the girlfriends, wives, celebs – and those which feature composite characters, or simple ciphers – those in which the *idea* is the important thing as regards their efficacy in getting the respondents off. It would also be worthwhile to see how many of the respondents who expressed interest in submission and domination seemed open to the idea of switching, since putting oneself in the place of the object of one's desire is half the fun of kinky behaviour, and perhaps no true dom, or tender one at any rate, is ever far from being a sub.

Curiosity permeates many of these fantasies, and those involving sexual thoughts about other men are far from all being grouped in chapter six. This is excluding group-sex situations where more than one man is present but they're not interacting sexually with each other, of course. I'm well aware that TV culture exists as a whole irrespective of whether individual TVs are gay or het. Some are liberated to express submissive or dominant tendencies more easily through cross-dressing (whether to be your bitch or whip your ass); some to express genderfuck, no-label beliefs; some are drawn to *becoming* the Other, the object of their desire. All of them would say they just get off on it. Nevertheless, TVs and TSs are headed here with the bi-curious because where they appear, more often than not, it's as a *straight* man's object of desire.

A quick plumb of the mental 'depths' reveals a few things I didn't receive any correspondence about, to speak of: I had only one respondent who briefly and unrealistically mentioned anal fisting. Outside the realm of porn stars, fisting of either kind is an intensely intimate experience best left to gamine lesbians with tiny wrists and hands. It has a violent sound because of the associations one makes with a fist, but in reality, excepting the gaping orifices of gonzo porn, is a slow, sensual, surgical-gloved experience that leaves the doer more captive than the done to. There were no amputees, no dwarves, no animals. There was no necrophilia, I'm very pleased to say, and – interestingly given the fact that it used to be a staple of pornographic literature at least in Roman Catholic Europe, from Dom B. to Georges Bataille – only one fantasy featuring religious imagery.

When it comes to the few who expressed their own tastes in porn, they lay one hundred per cent with the girl-next-door, Fiona Cooper or *Readers' Wives* styles of publishing, sluttish, spotty, irreverent, humourful and human. I didn't receive much in homage to flawless, perfect women. In fact the vast majority of respondents seemed to feel that it's the things that the beauty gurus of the media would consider *im*perfections, in which identity and individuality express themselves. Neither did I receive anything in homage to surgically enhanced frizzy-blonde porn stars or anything that reflected the influence of the bad-faith freakshow into which the excesses of porn can plunge.

Eight out of ten respondents, who expressed a preference, were into kinky sex! (That's a lot of cats.) And nearly eighteen per cent of respondents *think* – at least – about sex with other men. As I touched on above, the responses presented here are a mixture of fantasies, from the erudite to the functionally literate. The more confessional replies, however Walter Mittyish they may or may not be, were mostly elicited by the 'best sex you've ever had' wording of the survey. A few adopt a narrative style for ease of telling. The number of replies I received helpfully enclosing SAEs and asking what length I wanted the fantasy stories to be, if I had any plot guidelines, etc; and inquiries as to whether I wanted stories about their particular fantasy of, say, urolagnia; shows how unused men are to being asked about what they think about sex. Some respondents resolutely seemed not to grasp that I was actually asking them for what *they* thought about. Anyway, also presented here are three of the choicer offerings from among those fantasies that were presented in story form.

Frankly, I'm not sure if the contents of *My Secret Garden Shed* will reassure you as to the wholesome nature of men. But it will reassure you, if you feel the need, that however weird you think you may be, there's someone out there weirder than you!

And, unlike *My Secret Garden*, I *can* guarantee that this product is one hundred per cent dolphin-free.

2

Bread, Butter and Vanilla

Straight(ish) sex and sensuality

- This is where you'll find 'normal' sex, from missionary sex to group sex, swapping and 'dogging'.
- I've included a couple in this 'straight' section since their main focus is celebrity, even though they mention some kinky goings on!
- The majority of replies, though, emphasised the normality of their women – from the girl next door to the reader's wife, it seems that the likelihood of a good response is what we really want, and it's a game girl that really warms our cockles.
- On a poignant note, is it just me, or is there a touch of *Brief Encounter* wistfulness to the last one?

Male Sexual Fantasy in the 21st Century

THE QUESTIONNAIRE

What is your age? 48 years
Are you single, or in a long-term partnership or marriage? Single between longish-term relationships

23

but single merely means unmarried – your correct term should be 'playing the field'.

Are you . . . heterosexual? Yes.

What, if anything, do you find offensive? Please list things – objects, actions or even attitudes – which are to do with sex or which are often associated with sex and which offend you. In photographs, on television or in films:

- portraying certain male-female behaviour as biological when it's cultural
- sexist material
- double standards
- programmes that have tried to reverse this but exaggerated some points so much that they become unfair to men, e.g. *Sex and the City*

In novels: I only read non-fiction – can't comment.
In real life:

- male violence against women
- repressive attitudes (UK or USA versus Scandinavia or Italy)
- automatic male circumcision (still applied in the USA)
- men who won't use condoms to protect a woman's health
- women who say 'all men are the same' – we're not

Please fill in as much information in the following section as you wish. If you prefer to remain anonymous, that's fine. Name: anon. *Occupation:* Scientist

About your sexual fantasies (Definition: What you think about when you think about sex in such a way that you become sexually aroused): How often, on average, do you have sexual fantasies? A few times a week. More often between relationships than when in them.

Do your fantasies tend to have recurring themes or subjects? Yes. Or is each fantasy very different? Always similar; see below. If there are recurring themes or subjects, what are they?

- Casual, spontaneous sex with a stranger, often outdoors.
- In summer – deep in the woods or on a secluded beach, or in midwinter – outside, somewhere in the USA, both bathing in a large hot tub. Above us, snow falls steadily; below the water line, it's hot and steamy in every way. Little is spoken in these liaisons; who needs words? Just a growing stream of 'f' and 'c' words as we scale the heights of passion. Sometimes it's with a female friend/acquaintance with whom I can't imagine it occurring in reality.

Do you have a current favourite fantasy, or a fantasy that you enjoy more than most?

- This just happens to be the most recent. The first paragraph is true but the rest is fantasy. Late 2001, I went to a conference in Austria and on arrival I decided to dine in an Italian restaurant. While taking my order (neither of us spoke each other's language, we were both using our halting German) the waitress began to flirt like crazy with me and to stroke my left thigh. Somehow I couldn't take the gesture entirely seriously, as her boyfriend was at the other end of the room. Even so, there it was – tingling, throbbing arousal.

In my imagination only … after serving me a delicious meal and wine, she takes me to a private room next to the restaurant which is reserved not for the sensual pleasures of the table but for the sensual pleasures of the flesh. According to *The Joy of Sex,* the best Austrian restaurants used to have special rooms with a key on the inside, which couples could book. What does it matter that we don't speak each other's language? We share the language of bodily desire which is common to all humanity.

We lie down on a vast couch. She returns to fondling my thighs, strokes gently up my inner thighs, ever higher, to the point where desire becomes unstoppable; she sensually fondles my belly, neck *and beard*, we help each other to strip/tear off our remaining clothes and get to stroking each other everywhere – on her breasts, on my genitals, on hers, on my nipples, on her buttocks. The passion rises, and it doesn't stop but soars to unprecedented heights; literally, I've never seen it so hard, high and hot so early in an encounter.

We're entwined on the floor, we've rolled over again and I'm prostrate under a black-haired, dark-eyed Italian beauty whose intention is to fuck this visiting Englishman and give him all she's got. Her pussy's dripping all over me as she strokes and kisses my nipples, buttocks and anus, fondles my balls, stimulates my prostate and my other erogenous zones from head to toe. We writhe in passion; she's below me now, legs wide apart, desperate to be fucked. We get it in and we proceed to fuck, suck, caress and kiss for what could be an eternity but is probably less than twenty minutes, in which she has two small orgasms, a larger one and a final noisy, mind-blowing explosion in which her gasps and near-loss of consciousness precede by a few seconds my release of pent-up passion.

During a final minute of ecstasy, I virtually lose contact with the outside world and can only contemplate the looming, ever-nearer moment of irreversible climax. The feeling starts to spread all over me, from groin to brain, to the periphery of *my* limbs, of the most intense whole-body orgasm I've ever had. I penetrate her harder, harder, deeper, that urge common to all men, and start grunting and groaning so loudly that the whole restaurant must hear us. Finally, in more than a dozen earth-shattering spasms, my engorged balls and cock explode in glorious climax and a torrent of white-hot semen pours into her hungry cunt.

We lie back, temporarily sated, smiling, eyes expressing love, satisfaction and gratitude, kissing gently as our merged juices pour back out of her. Then, without a word, she motions me back on to the floor, gets on me in a sixty-nine position, belly to belly, with her head above my crotch and her beautiful pussy directly above my face (as in *The Joy of Sex* p. 173). She grabs the skin just above my balls and squeezes them away from my crotch, intensifying the exquisite sensation of renewed arousal.

Reciprocating the ecstasy, I start to lick, fondle and caress the pleasure spots between her legs but she motions me just to lie back and enjoy it. Struggling to keep me down, she licks, sucks and strokes me to a second, heart-stopping climax. I moan more loudly than before and drift into a spell of rising orgasmic ecstasy, the peak of pleasure that any human being on this earth will ever know, before erupting volcanically for a second time, but this time into her mouth. Slowly, as the muscular spasms subside, we reposition ourselves and I stimulate her with my lips and tongue to an equally delicious, equally final climax.

Well, just writing this all down has had a fairly stimulating effect. As with Nancy Friday's books, I hope that your book will help the causes of male–

female equality, sexual liberation and enjoyment for all.

About your sexuality: think back to when you were discovering your sexuality, your sexual orientation, and the sexual themes that are now part of your personality. What did you find erotic in those days? What things (for instance films, or books, or items of clothing) or people or experiences were a turn-on?

- School was a turn-off for shy intellectuals. Away at university in the early 70s, with kindred spirits, it was an immediate transition to an adult environment of responsibility, sexual freedom and liberation. *The Joy of Sex* was one of the leading texts. It's still not bad. The turn-ons that worked at 18 or 23 still work the same at 48. See above!

What things or people or experiences are particular turn-ons now?

- Written material. It's best if it's a volume which I haven't read before or which I last read years ago. Anything works – from 'erotica' to 'porn' but I suppose midway between the two is best. When I first opened one of Nancy Friday's books, the effect was instant.
- Visual material – films, videos, illustrations in educational books, or Channel 5 – all I can say is that happy couples or groups, passionately at it, work far better than 'porn' with undertones of violence or exploitation. Much of the best 'porn' just comes from people allowing others to photograph what comes naturally and I'd be happy if the other 'porn' disappeared tomorrow. In real life, I can't imagine a group scene, but in 'porn', it can be

a case of the more the simultaneous pleasure portrayed on screen, the better. Sound alone can work in real life; e.g. hearing another couple in the next-door hotel room once got us going.

- I'm surely not the only man to react positively to a pair of plump female buttocks. Women who are already slim don't realise that losing a further ten or twenty per cent of their weight could be to discard part of their sex appeal. To me anyway. Make-up, eye shadow, high heels, etc. are turn-offs. I tend to look for the real woman behind the mask. Why spend money on clothes? A plain T-shirt, sensually concealing a pair of breasts, can do more for me than the most expensive dress.

- Watching some sports or arts, even on TV, can be a pretty erotic ballet: women's swimming, etc. Sensually riding the crest of a wave, trying to prolong the peak of the experience.

- Alcohol always hastens the mood. Even caffeine. I'm less sure about cannabis. There's always a certain 'edge' to the best sex – an optimum level of tension? But women seem to need to be more relaxed.

Describe – in detail, don't be shy – the best sex you've ever had.

- Six years of it, in my late twenties/early thirties, with a partner who'd been brought up by broad-minded parents and was totally uninhibited. The first few months of this encounter were the best of all my life. A good match in other ways too. We always knew it might end if and when she finished her postdoctoral research in the UK. We're long separated by distinct careers, on different conti-nents.

What would improve your sex life?

- To have more courage/be less shy. Some opportunities in hindsight could have been bliss.
- A libido ten times higher. Knowing how often some men are in ecstasy – one can only believe what sex surveys say – the mind often wants a lot more than the body is capable of, although the body can sometimes be persuaded. I don't refer to a decline of libido with age – there isn't that much decline yet – rather it's always been a bit low and variable.
- Next time, a partner as good as the best I've ever had. The growth in specialist internet dating agencies is a big step towards more perfect matches and greater human happiness.

* * *

Dear Paul
I am replying to your advert in *Desire* magazine saying you want to hear fantasies which are filthy and bizarre. My name is R*****, a single white bisexual slut who is a huge fan of black men fucking white women. To me this is pure heaven. To me, Paul, there is no better sight in this world than to see a magnificent, very thick or long black penis fucking a white vagina, bumhole and mouth of a white woman and for her holes to be overflowing and dripping and flooded by hot black come from as many black knobs as possible. I will tell you my views and fantasies on black and white race relations and my own fantasies, and my very wild interracial fantasies for this country. I have views which would shock, horror and disgust many white people in this country.

I am a white guy who is a fanatical supporter of miscegenation, race mixing and the mass fucking and interbreeding of the white woman with the black man. I am also an anti-racist and see race mixing between black men and white girls and women as a real smack in the eyes for the white racists and bigots in this country or a type of wonderful sexual humiliation over this racist white rubbish in this nation. To me, Paul, it was the greatest thing ever to happen to this country when the blacks started to come here in their millions. I am a total supporter of mass black immigration and would love to see ten to fifteen million blacks let into these islands. This would lead to even more interracial sex and racial mixing and interbreeding between black and white. This would lead to my dream of a full-blown multicultural society ... black and white coming together, united in love and lust and united against the poison of racism. To me, Paul, it would be a total black and white multiracial and sexual revolution.

I am a very, very lucky guy, Paul, because what I support with so much passion is no longer a dream or a fantasy but beautiful black and white sexual reality. Interracial sex between black men and white women is booming in this country. Fifty per cent of black men have white girlfriends or wives, which I think is wonderful! I have nothing but love, affection and total support for the increasing number of white girls and women who are lovers of black men, black cock and spunk. These white females are free from the sickness of racism and hate. Many white women prefer black men to white, and once they have tasted black cock there is no going back.

I would love to see the black man in this country be the sexual master over the white man. I would mean my black brothers would have millions and millions of the most pretty, beautiful and stunning white women in these islands. Then I would want my black brothers in their millions to squirt their glorious jungle spunk into their cunts and wombs of millions of white ladies, putting them in the family way, making them pregnant. Nine months later, millions of white females in this nation would give birth to mixed-race, half-caste kids, their final product of interracial sex.

In this country so far, hundreds and thousands of white women have interbred with the black man. I call myself R***** the Race Mixer because of my fanatical support for miscegenation and interracial sex. I love living in this wonderful, multiracial country and then I think back to what it was like for black people over the years and centuries. Blacks were treated like shit by the white man and used as slaves and exploited and they had no human rights. This country was a boring white racist country which kept black people out. In the last fifty years, the walls of race and hate have been broken down, and black and white are mixing and coming together and fucking each other, mixing their black and white love juices with each other. When I think of the past and then what is happening today, it makes it all the more sweet. To me, black and white love is slowly defeating racism in this country, and I love it!

I have a very wild and bizarre fantasy which I would love to see become reality one day in London. It would be the staging of a huge black man/white woman naked march on a hot summer's day in the capital – about a million black men and white women. The white ladies just wearing their stockings and suspenders, high heels, showing their pussies and tits, holding hands with huge muscular black guys exposing their thick long black tools and glorious black ebony bodies. The march would end in Hyde Park, where there would be a huge rally. The speakers would be naked black men and white women. The speakers would be calling for more black immigration into this country and for more and more interracial sex and race mixing between black and white. The speakers would also be calling for the total sexual humiliation of the racist white male in this country by more and more black men, to take white girls and women, black cocks spunking into millions of white cunts, assholes and mouths.

After the rally a record-breaking open-air group sex party or orgy would take place between a million black brothers and white girls and women in Hyde Park. As these black stallions would fuck these white sluts senseless in their cunts, bumholes and mouths, all of these white whores would be gangbanged by large numbers of black studs and totally creamed and filled up with black cock juice, their hair, faces and bodies soaked and dripping in jungle seed. All of these white sluts would drink and swallow loads of Negro come, treating his sperm like the delicious nectar it is. I have tasted black spunk myself and would love to swallow as much as possible.

To me this whole march, rally and orgy of black man/white girl lust would be the most outrageous, decadent, beautiful and disgusting and shocking sight in the capital which would horrify and upset so many people as I would want. The whole event would be shown on national TV live all around this country. It would be an incredible sight as a million black brothers and white women would be fucking, sucking their brains out, the noise would be absolutely outrageous.

For my own fantasies, I am looking now for a black-loving white slut to be my wife and who I can share with black men. A white female who adores and loves the blacks and, like me, is a multiracist and race mixer. A white slapper who is addicted totally to black cock and spunk. I would encourage her to have as many black boyfriends and lovers as possible and to be fucked by eighty to one hundred black guys every year. She would be a slut who is very, very highly sexed and would be gangbanged by large numbers of black brothers. We would also hold black and white orgies in our house or in other places. We as a couple would really shock the neighbours as my white tart wife would be seen out with black guys, holding hands with them, dressed as a slut – very high heels, wearing sheer nylon stockings and miniskirts, showing her stocking tops, no undies. She would be often seen with groups of black guys and every day the neighbours would see different black men coming to the house. Sometimes groups, who she would let in. The locals would put two and two together, knowing she is being fucked and serviced by these black hunks when I am hard at work.

A revolution of interracial sex and race mixing is taking place in this country between millions of black men and white women and I love it!

No room for racists and racism in this country but room for millions of blacks to come here. I love black cock! And I am against racism.

Say no to racism and yes to black cock and spunk. I want millions of young white girls like this to become pregnant by the black man.

I want the black man in this country to totally humiliate the racist white man by taking and having all the white girls and women in this land.

* * *

I have often fantasised about what it would be like if my wife Maura and I were to have sex with another couple. I imagine we're on holiday in the Caribbean. We find ourselves sitting by the pool in our apartment complex alongside a couple in their late twenties. She's sunbathing topless, and I find myself getting an unexpected erection at the sight of her large breasts with their very pale nipples. I end up jumping into the pool to cool down, and as I swim a few splashy lengths, I notice that Maura has got talking to the couple. When I rejoin her, she introduces them as Richard and Mary, or whatever, from Surrey or wherever. As we talk, we find out we have a lot in common, and when Richard suggests that we go for a meal together that evening, Maura and I agree happily.

That night, we have a nice dinner in a local restaurant, and over a big jug of margarita, we find the conversation turning almost inevitably to the subject of sex. Thinking of Mary's firm tits as they had been displayed earlier that morning, I ask them if they had ever thought about swapping partners. Richard and Mary admit that not only have they thought about it, they have done it on several occasions, but it can be hard finding other couples who are amenable to the idea. Emboldened by the alcohol, I confess Maura and I are keen to try it.

'Come back to the apartment, then,' he says 'and we'll show you what to do.'

Maura and I are nervous but excited as they usher us into their apartment. There's a double and a single bed in the room, and Richard pushes them together to give us all the room we need. The French windows that lead to balcony are open, and we can hear the noise of the disco in the hotel's main block along with the chirping of insects in the bushes as Richard urges Maura to sit down on the bed and begins kissing and caressing. It feels strange to see my wife being fondled by this virtual stranger. Then Mary reaches for the zip on her dress and pulls it down before pushing the straps off her shoulders. Looking at her small, braless breasts, I'm beginning to get turned on. I feel Mary's hands around my waist as she reaches to pull my shirt free of my trousers and unfasten it. I relax into her embrace.

Soon, Maura is lying on the bed wearing nothing but her G-string, and Richard's head is bent over her as his mouth feasts on hers. She's moaning softly, and her hand moves to cup her pussy through her panties and stroke it. Mary breaks away from me. 'Let me do that,' she murmurs, and I watch, mesmerised, as she pulls down my wife's panties. I can see that the pussy lips are already swelling, a damp patch clearly visible on the gusset of the stringy panties as Mary lobs them into the corner. I know that Maura has never been touched intimately by another woman before, and I half expect her to protest as Mary's fingers begin to probe her juicy cunt, but she seems to relish what's being done to her. I strip off quickly, eager to join the tangle of bodies on the bed, and then get behind Mary. She's wearing a halter-necked top, a cut I've always liked, and I untie it, giving myself access to those big, succulent breasts. As she continues to play with my wife's pussy, I roll her nipples between my fingers and thumbs, feeling them go hard beneath my touch.

When Mary slides two fingers deep into my wife's cunt, I know Maura is ready to be fucked. Richard has sensed it, too, and undressed. As he slips down his briefs to reveal his cock, I notice that while it's no longer than mine, it's very thick, and the thought of it stretching Maura's pussy wide makes my own penis twitch with envy and excitement.

Richard urges Maura up on to all fours, and I realise he's going to fuck her doggy-style. That is probably her favourite position, and I knew she would really appreciate the feel of that fat shaft as Richard thrust into her. She groans as she tries to accustom herself to its unexpected girth, and I give my own cock a few swift rubs as I watch Richard gradually ease himself home. I don't have too long to enjoy the spectacle, though, before Mary has dropped to her knees and taken my erection between her wet, skilful lips. I watch Richard give my wife a good shafting and luxuriate in the feeling of the languid blow job I'm getting from Mary. She knows exactly what she's doing, and as her tongue moves in wicked little circles over the head of my prick I know it won't be too long before I come. She must realise how close I am getting to coming, because she suddenly spits on my cock and tells me to lie down on the bed. The next moment, she's straddling my body, her quim enveloping my hard-on as tightly as her mouth had done. As she bounces up and down the six inches, I'm able to reach up and maul her breasts, squeezing them with my fingers as she moans in a mixture of pain and ecstasy. Her cunt muscles milk my cock, and while Richard continues to fuck Maura with increasingly rapid strokes, I give up and come inside Mary's sweet cunt.

Maura's throaty little cries indicate that she's in the throes of her own orgasm, and as I lie recovering, Mary uses her own fingers to bring herself off. Richard groans and announces that he's coming. He gives one last, hard jerk, and then pulls out of Maura's body to let the last spurts of his come spatter over her ass cheeks. To my surprise and delight, Mary pushes her husband out of the way and sets about licking her husband's come off Maura's backside, before moving lower to push her tongue into my wife's cunt. She's licking the mixture of Richard's spunk and Maura's love juices up with relish. Maura relaxes on the bed, and lets Mary give her a thorough tonguing. From the smile on her face it's clear she's enjoying every moment of what's being done to her. When Mary turned round over Maura's body, so that her sex was an inch from my wife's face, Maura merely sticks out her tongue and began to sample the taste of Mary's gauzy pussy for the first time.

'It's a beautiful sight, isn't it?' Richard says in my ear. 'Two people of the same sex enjoying each other's body, I mean.' I have barely had time to register his words before I feel his hand reach down and grasp my cock, which has begun to stiffen again at the sight of the two women in the sixty-nine position. 'That's the great thing about being on holiday,' Richard muttered as he begins to wank me with smooth, efficient strokes. 'You can do anything you want, be anything you want – and no one will ever find out.' His touch on my cock is skilful, his other hand coming down to cup and gently stroke my balls. When he urges me to get on the bed, in the same kneeling position my wife had so recently adopted to receive him, I do not object. I see him spit on his hand, using his own saliva to lubricate his shaft, then I feel his wet tongue rimming my asshole. I enjoy the sensation, and turn my head to watch my wife lying beside me, her mouth working hungrily on Mary's hairy quim. I feel something warm and hard replace Richard's tongue at the entrance to my anus, and know it is the head of his cock. I relax, doing all I can to ease his entry, pushing outward with my anal muscle, almost crying out as his glans breaches my virgin ass. Within seconds, the pain in my ass subsides and is replaced with the first spasmings of pleasure as he buries himself in me to the hilt. As Mary and Maura moan and sigh and move towards their orgasms, Richard begins to fuck me with strong, steady strokes. I reach down and wank my own cock in time to Richard's thrusts. All too soon, we're both coming, my spunk arcing out powerfully enough to hit the bedstead. Mary was more than happy to lick both of us clean, and then the four of us fall asleep, curled up together on the bed. In my fantasy, Maura and I get together with the couple almost every night of that holiday. I've not discussed this with my wife, but I'd love to see such a fantasy become reality. I suppose that's why I think about being on holiday – it would give us a licence that perhaps we don't have at home.

* * *

Beautiful Creature
You know how the celebrities you get in all those magazines like *Hello*, *OK* and *People* are so well-scrubbed, squeaky-clean, germ-free? Well it makes me want to fuck them much more than I do someone who's being sluttish. I've nothing against women being 'up-front about their sexuality', and like most men I'm a total tart myself, so I can respect that. That's just it I suppose: I can respect that, maybe too much. But women who present themselves as so polished, like their shit don't stink, as they say? I just want to defile them, to rub their face in it. Or at least, muzz up their hair.

Kate Winslet is a good example – she has this English Rose image, and OK, she's doing the Hollywood thing now, but back when she was in all those Britflicks like a total drama student, she had this girl-next-door thing. She's really wholesome, and yet, if you look closely, she's got this really cruel twist to her lips. It's refreshingly out-of-its-time, with all the rosy collagen pouts around these days. Her lips curl just as they would were she about to smash a cane down against my bad-boy ass. Those lips look like they know a thing or two between smiling for the paparazzi on some red carpet in LA. They look as I think they would were her head thrashing around beneath me as I arc over her, plunging into her, transporting her, her hair thatching the pillow to either side, her eyes rolled back and those lips trembling. Wonder if her clit would quiver in quite the same way?

* * *

Britney Baby, One More Time

I have a fantasy about Britney Spears. She comes across as so knowing, but in all those interviews craps on about her virginity. Her first hit single was that one with the video of her and the dancers in a high school, in those dancer's versions of British school uniforms. Then there was the one with her in a red PVC catsuit, all polished up and shining under the lights, pulling tightly where it counts, and all the time her singing so unassumingly, not owning up to being sexy.

In my fantasy, I'm a stinky old homeless person (which I'm not). I've been sleeping rough for ages and I can smell myself. A mingled and almost unbearable odour of filthy clothes and flesh assaults my nostrils. I've got a matted beard. One day, in a trashcan in downtown San Francisco, Union Square where the homeless line up for the soup kitchens, I find among the hero wrappers and sticky old papers a large, shiny reel of recording tape, the old kind that only professionals use these days. I know enough about bands and stuff to know I'm looking at an original master tape, and on the flange I see there's a sticker, Britney

– *Steal Me Baby One More Time*. Thinking that this must be worth a few bucks at least to some internet geeks' Britney auction or something, I tuck it beneath my arm and head off to put it in the safe place where I keep things I don't want others to know about, making up my mind to find out about those things.

Later, I've returned to my pitch near where other homeless hang out, when suddenly I hear a commotion down the street from me. Looking distraught, a petite young girl, no more than the teen she is in reality, rushes up to me in tight, flared pants and a tight top cut to show off the tight stomach beneath it, and I realise it's Britney. On her own, in a panic, she's ditched her minders. I affect not to recognise her. Wiping her eyes and sniffling, she asks me, 'Mister, have you been here most of the day?'

'Nowhere else to go, Lady,' I mumble with an affected coolness.

'In that case, you seen a reel of recording tape? About so . . .' she gestures suggestively with her hands '. . . big?'

Seizing the moment, I throw her the bait. 'Might have. Was it important?'

She makes that impatient clicking sound that Valley Girls make. 'Nu-uh. Just, like, the master of my latest track – real valuable, that tape.' Then her face clears, and she frowns right at me. 'Say – you know where it is, don't you?'

Ignoring her question, I tell her, 'Worth a lot of money to me too, and what I get for it will mean more to me than it does to you!' Softening my tone, I gesture at my greasy fly and pat it, 'and you tell me, young lady, you want to see something *you* haven't seen before?'

To my own amazement, she halts for a second, taken aback, then smiles. 'I get it. Yeah, but where could we go? You're homeless, right? And my people would just think it was retarded!'

Without delay, I reach out for her hand. 'I know a place – c'mon.'

'And I'll get the tape back, right?' Turns out that for a long time, young Britney's been straining at the leash of her management. She loves her career – but all the self-discipline and carrot juice gets too much at times. And she has to be a good girl the whole time, can't go necking in cars like her peer group. If you're just Jane Doe, who cares if someone thinks you're a slut from time to time? But that sort of thing could ruin Britney. So it turns out that by blackmailing her I'm giving her the excuse not to take responsibility for her actions. And she thinks, being an old homeless guy, I don't know who she is, so she's getting to escape from her fame for a while, too. And I'm not letting on. So there, on my old mattress in a disused warehouse, Britney goes wild. She goes down on me, unzipping my filthy old pants with a rasp and fellating me, a sheen of sweat on her clear young skin, her blonde hair falling across her face. She takes a bunch of it in one fist and pauses to caress my shaft with it. Then she builds the pace again until I spatter her face with my come.

Turning over, she presents her perky ass to me. Her pants are already off one leg, and pool around the knee of the other as she kneels on the stained mattress, reaching her fingers through her legs to play with her clit. She gets off like that, wiping her face back and forth against the mattress, rubbing my spunk into her face and muzzed-up hair, muttering about how it's good for her complexion as I lay recovering behind her. With the view, it doesn't take long to stiffen again and I steer my cock towards her cunt. Suddenly, I feel a hand shoot up to cover her entrance. 'Not there,' Britney whispers hurriedly. 'That's for my husband. Higher.' Slowly, I grasp her meaning. Her ass is well lubricated. She's so turned on by being with this stinky old hobo that her juices have run the length of her crack. I notice a few zits around her ass – must be the heat inside those red catsuits. My cock pops easily into her tight hole and my hands reach round to cup her glorious tits.

With that, we usually roll and tumble in my mind until I'm done! Her on top, giving me a tit-job, whatever. As she leaves, hours later with the master tape tucked under her arm, having wiped the last of my spunk from her pneumatic body and smoothed down her hair as best she can, she turns and says, 'Listen Mister, you may not realise it, but you've just made a lot of young music fans happy, and you've made *this* young musician *very* happy.'

* * *

My Dream of Madonna

I was tossing and turning, half-dreaming my way into wakefulness. The telephone rang. Before it had finished its third ring, I picked up the receiver.

'Hello, Honey; you got through.'

I sensed the voice with an etheric shudder. It was hers and no other's. It must have been that chain letter, or that very special message on the contact line.

'We've got to meet. Midnight at the cathedral. Look your best; be your best!'

So it was going to happen: Madonna would approve me, fulfil me. I was all a-tremble. I hurriedly shaved, showered and dressed. I looked intellectually smart-casual in dark brown cords. What the hell ? Whatever fashion I chose, Madonna was sure to do some really imaginative permutations.

I went down to the vestibule, meaning to call a cab. There, waiting for me, were her bodyguards – tall, coffee-coloured, muscular hunks, role models for my work-outs.

'Hi! We've come to collect you. This is your honour and ours.'

They ushered me into a plush Chevrolet. The engine purred, in time with my quivering anticipation. *I was going to be a sex-object for Madonna.*

The cathedral's columns tapered into the infinite darkness, like seductive limbs in erotic dress. The bodyguards motioned me to go in, then turned and left.

The interior was swathed in dim red light. I could hear the dulcet sounds of a choir, singing something like Gregorian chant. But no singers were to be seen. I looked ahead, towards the altar. There, in two lines, were twelve beautiful girls, all the same height, about five foot eight. They were wearing white silk robes with pink sashes. They beckoned me to kneel at the altar, then to stand up.

The lights dimmed. Then, from the rear, Madonna entered. She looked exquisite in a purple velvet ball gown, glittering with a handful of jewels flashing all primary colours, revealing her shoulders, so wonderfully toned by all her sensual exercise. Her hair was now black and straight, her complexion fresh, without make-up. She stood between the two rows of girls. Then she smiled at me. 'You're looking great,' she said 'I must see more.'

She lifted her arms in the air and nodded at the girls. The one on the far left undid her sash, parted her robe, and pushed it back over her shoulders. It fell to the floor to reveal the girl's athletic body, tightly encased in a white girdle and a black bra-top. She came and undid my jacket, then bore it away.

Each girl did the same with one more item of my clothing. Madonna's eyes gradually lit up as my body was revealed to her. At last I stood before her, just wearing black briefs. Madonna was feasting at the sight of my torso and legs. Our faces edged together. Our lips touched, then drew our tongues together as we held our breath through a five-minute kiss.

'Wonderful,' she whispered. 'Could you help me with my preparations now?'

Now I was to undress Madonna! I went up to the altar, put my hands on her slender waist, and looked her straight in the eye. The gown had a zip at the back. I undid it and eased it down. As it fell to the floor, it captured a moment of eternity. The song resounded in my ears: *close my eyes; Oh God, I think I'm falling, out of the skies, close my eyes.* I did the same with her diaphanous slip. Now she was in crisp white linen underwear. How liberated I felt, body and soul

'Well done,' she said, 'and now there are some further delights.' She disappeared through a door at the back. There was a tap on my shoulder. It was one of the bodyguards.

'Come this way!'

He led me through a side door and down a long dark corridor. We emerged into a dazzling chamber – like an eighteenth-century palace, with gold lacquered walls, masses of mirrors and divan couches. At the far end was a glass door, and through this door an enormous swimming pool. I knew what was to come. One of the other bodyguards turned up beside me, with a pile of clothes.

'You must get changed,' he said, 'then the rest is up to you'. They both left me.

I looked at the gear. There was a white bathrobe, a singlet top, a pair of shiny black boxer shorts and two pairs of trunks – one 50s style, hip-height, navy blue with a white waistband, the others much briefer, with a leopard-skin pattern.

That was great: I find fifties swimwear a great turn-on because it holds a bit of allure and suspense of forbidden fruit. Good to have this when the fruit is no longer forbidden. And super-liberated women of the here and now like something briefer as well. So why not combine the two?

Madonna came in, covered in her wrap. 'Let's flex a few muscles first,' she said. We took off each other's wraps. Madonna was now in a schoolgirl's gym skirt and singlet top. We did a few minutes' press-ups together. Then Madonna pulled me upright to face her. 'Time for some waves together.'

We pulled each other's tops off, Madonna first. Then she pulled down my shorts. 'Down to your trunks, Darling,' she breathed. *From Here to Eternity* – where are we now? Madonna twinkled with delight. She was so beautiful for me, she made me feel so beautiful. The gym skirt uncapped and unzipped with ease.

Madonna before me in her bathing costume: what a revelation! It froze eternity, made time stop in its tracks with the accentuation of her lovely breasts and hips. It was a gorgeous white Jantzen number with boned bra, like in the *Reveal Yourself* poster. How often I had been bowled over by that poster, and those Esther Williams movies; and now I was in the action!

She took me by the hand and led me to the pool. She jumped in first and did the backstroke – so I could see her breasts and thighs thrusting up through the water. Wow: if I could live to tell how it felt! I'd just caught a second's glimpse of her swimming in the *Erotica* video. How long I had yearned for more.

Now here it was. I jumped in with her. I don't know how many lengths we did together. There was a Lilo floating in the middle of the pool. We lay on it together. Our embraces made ripples on the pool's edge. We went to the pool's side. It was quite hot, so our bodies and our costumes dried quickly.

Again she took me by the hand, and led me back to the chamber. She pulled down my trunks. Hmm: the second pair were even more of a turn-on for her. I unzipped her costume at the back, and peeled it down. Now I saw her whole body, so beautifully revealed, toned to perfection by that exercise.

She stripped me naked, and led me to an ample couch.

Erotic; erotic; Put your hands all over my body!

We did it all, both ways. Making love to Madonna led me to the heights of the heavens; deep into the bed of every ocean. We were each other's waterfalls. We opened up the portals of all life's energies, generated all, conquered the world in the name of the purest, deepest sensual love.

Madonna lay back on the couch. 'You met my challenge to the full,' she said, 'You probably read about me that my personal religion gave me a wonderful inner strength. I've just shared that strength with you, built that strength in you. Now the world is yours.'

As we reflected on our accomplished ecstasy, a group of six boys and six girls came into the chamber. The boys were attired in boxer shorts, the girls in gym skirts and singlet tops. They could almost have come from *Baywatch,* though they were perhaps a little leaner.

'We want to learn from your example' they said.

'OK,' replied Madonna, 'just line up in couples, then approach us, couple by couple.' This they did.

Madonna stripped each boy down to his trunks – black, 50s-style. I stripped down each girl to reveal a gorgeous purple Jantzen one-piece.

We regaled ourselves on seeing their lovely, glowing, healthy bodies go into delicious swimsuit embraces, and then bared to wonderful abandoned consummation. Their joyous massed orgasm lifted us again above the stratosphere, with an extra rocket blast from all humanity. Universally recharged, we made love again, rapturously, delicately modulating all the masculine and feminine sides of our natures. It was great that my anima could melt out into her. The choir's remote airs lilted above us in our euphoria.

Madonna and I had done it, inspired and radiated our message to humanity.

Madonna, you have set me *free*!

* * *

Action Woman
One thing that really attracts me is women being active. I don't think it means I'm a submissive man, particularly, I think it's more something like wanting to spar with them. I either like women who reach the extremes of human endeavour, like single-handed yachtswomen (I kind of like anoraks, actually. The way they wrap people up. Then there's all those guy ropes and webbing.), or I just like women doing the everyday. But not the traditional things, the cooking and ironing, etc. Women driving, for some reason, have always turned me on. Any woman almost – I think it's something about the driving itself. When I was at school, I used to get a lift from my best mate's mum, and I used to glance over and watch her from the front seat. I loved the way the strap of the seatbelt bisected her tits, and the other one made her stomach

look trim; the way she turned the wheel; the way she'd bite her lip when she was judging an intersection. Most of all perhaps, it was the way her legs were always slightly split, stretching her skirt to the seams, to operate the pedals.

I still look for these things whenever I drive with a woman. My girlfriend ends up driving sometimes when I've had a drink and, especially if I'm a bit inebriated, I love to look over and look for these things. I'm in danger of pawing her and distracting her from driving, in fact. I wish a man could go down on a woman who's in a driving position as satisfyingly as a woman can a man, in fact! And whenever I get a lift with a woman – at work or wherever – I'm always intrigued by how they drive, and whether or not it turns me on. Another active thing I really like is women in bands. I love the idea that, however intellectual their band is, they're really just performing, showing themselves off. And watching is a privilege – one that women have almost had to themselves in pop music since Elvis. I loved it when bands like Elastica and Hole came along. Here were women cavorting like rock guys, sweating like pigs, and really putting it on the line. I suppose I just love to see women *doing* things. It's hardly surprising, because you get to know who they are then.

I'm not really very kinky in real life, although I've nothing against it. And I've never really played computer games, having a life as I do. I don't know much about film stars either, so know nothing about Angelina Jolie who plays her, but something about the idea of Lara Croft turns me on. It's that gymnastic thing I suppose, the way you could really imagine cavorting with her between the sheets – legs and arms everywhere. Although her body's a bit masculine, in a way. I'd love to play paintball against a real woman like that – and win, of course, lobbing paint pellets at her rear end, tight in its khaki, pinning her down and splattering her, on her chest, against the visor of her mask, watching her kick and struggle to throw me off.

In fact, I can imagine myself in some real guerilla war-type scenario, where rules are out of the window, and Lara's the enemy. She runs out of ammo and, after a chase through the sweltering jungle, me and a couple of the other faster guys from my unit catch her. We pin her down, although she spits in our faces and kicks like a mule. We have to tie her up with bits of jungle twine to stop her taking her own life, so spirited is she. Anyway, the point of this fantasy is that, to get the location of her comrades out of her, I imagine her being staked out – as her sweat soaks through her khakis – over a bed of bamboo, to make her talk. I think it's something that captured my imagination in one of those old small-format *Battle* comics you used to get when I was a kid, where they'd have stories about the Japanese in World War II. The stuff grows so fast and so stiffly, apparently, that you'd only need to be stretched over it for hours before it hurt. Depending on how freaked out I am by thinking about this, because I could never hurt someone in real life, even if they wanted me to probably, I think, I imagine to varying degrees that she's somehow reassured, or has a get-out, like her unit will have moved on, and she can tell us what she knows without any harm, or something. But I guess something appeals to me about having someone like her as my prisoner in a way I hadn't thought about for ages until I did this letter! Merry Christmas, Ms Croft!

* * *

I would like to tell you about what happened the time my wife's best friend, Loz, came to stay for the weekend. Linda and Loz have known each other since they were six, and though their lives have taken very different paths – Loz went to university and has a job working for a TV production company in London, while Linda and I got married when she was just nineteen and she works locally – the two have remained very close. Loz rang Linda to tell her that she had just split from her boyfriend of three years and was very down about it. Linda immediately invited her down to visit us, in the hope it would cheer her up. Loz arrived on the Friday night, and after dinner and a couple of bottles of wine between the three of us, she and Linda sat talking while I sat watching the football highlights on TV, letting the girls get on with it. I always had a soft spot for Loz. She is by far the most attractive of all my wife's friends, with her shoulder-length blonde hair, and heart-shaped slim yet curvaceous figure. I hated to see her quite so depressed. When Linda and I got into bed, I was in the mood for sex, and I ran my hand lightly down to cup one of her big breasts through her nightdress. Linda responded, and soon her nightie was in a heap on the floor and the two of us were lying on top of the duvet, my fingers between her legs and stroking her rapidly moistening sex. She, in turn, was wanking my cock to its full seven-inch length, and once she was ready to take it inside her, she straddled me and lowered her pussy on to my rigid cock. We had completely forgotten about Loz, who was sleeping on the sofa bed in the lounge, as Linda bounced up and down on my cock, sighing and moaning. I have to admit she is pretty noisy when she comes, and as I gave one hard jerk of my hips and my penis shot its load of spunk up into her, she was probably shrieking like a banshee, although neither of us were aware of it at the time.

Satisfied, Linda rolled off me, curled up under the duvet and was soon asleep. However, I was finding it hard to drop off since, as is frequently the case after sex of course, I badly needed to piss. I slipped out of bed and pulled on my dressing gown, then turned on the hall light and padded down the hallway to the bathroom. The lounge in our flat is opposite the bedroom, and as I walked past I noticed the door was slightly ajar, and that the light was still on. I also thought I could hear a faint sobbing sound. Wondering if Loz was all right, I popped my head quietly round the door, and saw the most erotic sight I think I have ever seen. Loz was lying on the sofa bed, the covers pushed back. She was stark naked and it was immediately obvious that she was masturbating. Her left hand was cupping her small, firm tit, her fingers playing with the nipple, while her other hand was working something in and out of her pussy.

I should have gone straight to the bathroom, but I was transfixed by what Loz was doing. She had not shown any sign that she was aware of my presence; her head was hanging over the edge of the sofa bed and her eyes were closed. I realised that what she was thrusting into herself was one of the large candles which we keep on the mantelpiece as decoration. Her hips were bucking as she fed more and more of the candle into her wet cunt. It was such a beautiful sight to watch that I could not help letting out a groan of pure lust. The noise was enough to bring Loz to her senses and she turned her head to see me silhouetted in the doorway.

Scowling, she pulled the candle out of herself with a sudden sucking sound and made to pull up the bed, but I shook my head. 'Please, carry on,' I urged. 'You look so horny, I want to watch you.' She hesitated for a moment, then beckoned me into the lounge, motioning to me to shut the door behind me. I did as she asked and stood there, my reawakened erection strong enough to tent the folds of my dressing gown. I was rewarded by the sight of Loz pushing the candle slowly back into her sex, then using both hands to force it in and out. She was making sweet little whimpering noises as she moved closer to her climax, then her body seemed to convulse as her muscles closed hard around the fat waxy taper, not in the least put off by her audience!

When she had recovered from her shattering orgasm, she told me that the rhythmic squeaks and cries of Linda and I fucking had made her feel so horny and frustrated particularly as she was badly missing the active sex she had enjoyed with her boyfriend, that she had wanted not just a wank but to be filled, and that the only thing she could do was use the candle to bring herself off. We hadn't touched and the whole thing had been chance. There was no reason to feel guilty towards the woman who was my wife and her best friend, and we agreed to keep the event a secret. I was so turned on – again – by what I had just watched that I went straight back into the bedroom, woke Linda and fucked her for a second time. She asked what had got into me, but how could I tell her that it was poor sad Loz who had got me so aroused? Since then I have fantasised about nothing else.

3

Light Relief

Playful perversions and kinky fun

- Here you'll find most of the porn-literate replies – people who are familiar with the different genres and clichés of erotica and porn, and use them referentially.
- Come in trawler man, your time is up. Time to stop fishing. A nation's women are looking for a man like you!

Since you ask, and I can't think that anyone else ever has (having lived a very quiet and bookish life and well on into the second half of it):

I would think that I have had sexual intercourse less than a fifth, perhaps less than a tenth, of the number of times I have wanted it. I lost my virginity far too late, I was brought up to think of sexual experience – if at all – as an optional extra, I don't think I have even masturbated or had sexual fantasies enough, and to a great extent regret the quiet and bookish temperament which, together with much ill health of various sorts, has meant that this first sentence is true – I am unusual, but in a minority. Not unique, there must be many approximately like me.

Favourite fantasies: I am living somewhere warm in a moderately big house, I keep three or four young or very young (late teenage) women there much as I now keep dogs. I give them food and exercise (especially tennis), educate them somewhat, but provide no clothes. They are always naked, it's pleasant for me but so usual it's like having pretty wallpaper; I too am most of the time naked. Since (in this dream) it is miserable to go to sleep or to wake up without an erection, I sleep between two of them, fondling Miss Left at night while Miss Right plays with my prick and balls. Miss Right in the morning ... I remember my manners and while I am always making comparisons mentally, do not speak them aloud. Each afternoon, outdoors I have full intercourse with a third, the fourth that day attends to cooking and other domestic tasks. By some kind of rota I have much variety.

Another: I'm aged twenty plus. It's the 50s and I imagine myself to have just graduated, and to have called on an older rich relation, a doctor who is partly crippled, to get summer employment. After some chat, since it is very hot he tells me to go down the big garden and have a swim in the big pool there, making me feel faintly prudish when he brushes aside my objection that I have no swimming costume with me. I will find towels. I have never swum naked before, after fifteen minutes he appears in his wheelchair pushed by his grey-uniformed and very pretty employee, orders me to come out and be examined if I want a job. When I object he says that the girl is a nurse and will take no notice. I am (in my imagination), as he comments, a very strong and well-set-up

young fellow. He – I nearly control my embarrassment – holds my testicles to test for ruptures. 'What
do you think?' he says to her. 'I want to see it up,'
she answers, and takes her slightly uneven breasts out
of her dress. Though I am not a virgin my sexual
experiences have been in dark corners and though I
have felt breasts I have never seen them. I am
immediately erect. She approves. I am employed that
summer, because my uncle can no longer have
intercourse or masturbate much, to have intercourse
or to be masturbated either by him or by her or both
to amuse them. Now I am old and imagine myself
rich I wonder whether to employ a young couple for
much the same purposes, and decide against it. I
remember that summer not as being in any way
degrading, but restrictive, never believing myself free.

Minor fantasies: aged twenty or so masturbating a
male friend, having him do so to me; aged fifty
masturbating a younger man, tall, strong and muscular, perhaps black; sunbathing naked with a female
friend who will not mind if I have an erection (come
to think of it I have done that); remembering
swimming naked rather than doing it, which after the
first though very beautiful moments turned out to be
much like swimming with a costume; swimming
naked with an erection which I have done once, like
fucking the sea. I'm not much interested in supposedly sexy costumes and revolted by anything to do with
assholes, but what was hinted at in the Stephen Fry
film about Oscar Wilde where they were face to face,
rubbing erections together? Don't think I would
enjoy that much but I'd like to try it once. I've several
times (but can never quite remember it) had sex in a
posture I've never seen in any book, so that my
testicles can be played with at the same time. I think
some of the postures I've seen in pictures look

uncomfortable or impossible. I play with myself sometimes – play? No, it's worth taking seriously – according to the penis-strengthening exercises in a book on tantric yoga I have – finishing by holding the erection lightly at the top with one hand, stroking it with the other twenty times. The book says start with ten. Other fantasies: a woman with auburn hair, blue eyes, pale skin; a brunette ditto; a woman with a great deal of chestnut pubic hair; yoga teachers; gym mistresses; hockey players; (Curlers? No, perhaps not!); Researching and writing a book called *Around the World in Eighty Whores*.

In fact I lead a sober life, rarely have intercourse, do not masturbate much, have thought but only thought of going to massage parlours (though I don't know the prices I doubt if I could afford them), wonder sometimes about finding an obliging much younger woman. (How? Where? Not such a fool as to think that she wouldn't prefer a man of her own age.) I swim naked when I can, not often, alone in the early morning, sauna naked if the choice is there (But how very few men take this option! The local leisure centre has ceased its 'men only' times for lack of patronage, and its 'women only', for the same reason, I suppose.) I have never swum naked with other men except in American YMCAs where the atmosphere was bleak.

So I'm obsessed with nakedness and masturbation more than with intercourse, probably because they're easier to come by and because, well, I enjoy it.

* * *

I'm not sure if my fantasy is sensual or bizarre, or simply middle of the road, either way I do know my grammar, spelling and punctuation are not up to much so forgive me, but here goes.

My fantasy is a role-play scenario that begins with myself being subservient but eventually becoming dominant, and it revolves around me being a slave during Roman times. The centurions are off fighting, expanding the Roman Empire, their wives surrounded simply by eunuchs and ladies in waiting.

A wife of an extremely wealthy and successful officer is left to entertain herself inside their opulent villa. Set in relative isolation, in its own vineyards, but close enough to Rome itself for the wife to organise soirées with other soldiers' wives. They chat – four or five of them one evening. The talk eventually gets round to how long their husbands are away, and how frustrating it is for them sexually. The talk gets raunchier, they talk of gadgets/gizmos until one woman tells of a tale she'd heard, where once a week, a wife gives her eunuchs the night off, as well as the maids. She calls three friends over and they go down into her dungeon where she has four slim, handsome men, handcuffed and manacled to a wall. They are all naked, and blindfolded. Where did she get them from, one asked. 'From the marketplace, bought them with a view to making them eunuchs, but snuck them into her lair. The maids were sworn to secrecy, with a murderous fate awaiting them if they breathed a word. It was the maids' job to clean up and feed the men.

So they all stripped off and they decided to have their own Olympics. Each woman would line up in front of a slave. They would then, with just the use of their mouths and tongue, see who could make their own chosen slave come first, the proof being a face full of cream. I hear them drink, sing and shout. They then get the men from standing up to lying down, they each swap men, straddle the new faces, commanding them to keep their mouths open, whereupon

they proceed to see who can pee first and longest over
the slave. After this they remain where they are and
simply wank themselves off, either using their own
fingers, or in most cases by lowering themselves down
on to the man's mouth, lips, nose, face in general
where they will either tell the slave to lick away or
they will rub themselves over his face. I hear one poor
slave nearly died as one of the women was having
such a good time, rubbing her clitoris all over his
mouth and nose, that he nearly suffocated, he only
survived because she eventually came. Well, you can
imagine not only are the slaves well and truly erect
but the women are craving some cock inside them,
and so the next competition begins, who can ride the
slave until he comes first. It might seem unfair on the
one who already came earlier when being sucked off
you might think, but I'm told they just keep sucking
until they all come, so astride they sit, all in rows next
to each other. The wine is still being drunk and
spilled. Their talking is becoming filthy and blatant –
'fuck me harder, slave,' – that kind of thing, as they
egg each other on. No one is sure who comes first, the
slaves or the women, but I do know they all orgasm,
fucking the slaves for as long as it takes. I heard one
week one of the ladies got so drunk she sat down on
a slave's cock so quickly she missed and it went right
up her ass. After the initial shock I'm told that she
loved it so much that's all she does now, cocks up her
bum whilst fingering/rubbing her clit. All this went on
for months until one week they were all so drunk they
forgot to shut the clasps on one man as they were
changing them round from standing up to lying
down. He didn't let on at first, just waited his time
then when they were all pretty drunk, slipped his
blindfold off, grabbed the nearest woman and
chained her up. It happened so quickly they didn't

realise. They soon sobered up and he did a deal: he wouldn't bring attention to the house provided they paired up and licked each others' pussies. They then rimmed each other, after which they finger-fucked each others' assholes until such time as they could fist each other. At first they refused, but he hollered out. They shushed him and the first pair got together and after much lubrication one woman was ready to be fisted. The slave took over, fisting one with his left hand while one woman sucked on his balls. While his cock was fucking and a third was in her mouth, the fourth stood in front of him while he periodically licked her pussy/clit, and watched the rest of the action. He kept this up until he exploded his own come down the throat of the cock-sucker. He then continued to fist the one girl until she came. I heard that the women were shocked but all so delighted and satisfied that they all did a deal. I'll let you guess what the deal was . . .

Well that's it. I feel Romans, their myth and lifestyle, is very important in adding to the stimulus, it's not a tale of bondage per se and it's not about either males or females having continual control over the other. It's about finding sexual equality through mutual satisfaction, albeit accidentally, no matter what form it takes. Anyway, I apologise for the presentation, but I find writing it in letter form more erotic than typewriter or computer. I think that the action is finite, but I feel building up the minutiae is what makes the story horny.

*　*　*

I have seen your advertisement in the current issue of *Forum*, seeking sexual fantasies. I have pleasure in enclosing one of mine, one of many I have, being a bisexual fetish exhibitionist. If you should like to read about my others, I would be only too pleased to forward them.

Carolyn is in her forties, tall, slender, with an auburn bob, gorgeous and, oh, before I forget to mention it, classy. The word 'class' was, I think, invented for her. Estranged from her wealthy husband, the children – not children any more – at university, she is all alone in that large house in the suburbs.

We used to work together, I *always* had a thing about her, which never amounted to anything but slow, luxurious wank sessions in my bedroom, Carolyn's rubber-catsuited figure etched in my mind. I doubt she ever wore rubber, but it is my fantasy, after all.

I meet her in the club, where I go every week. I am dressed, as per usual, in some kinky outfit, this time a bulging leather jockstrap, chained and studded, steel and leather wrist straps, slave collar and leash, studded boots and leather waistcoat. I bump into Carolyn, almost, on the passage from one room to another. She eyes me up and down, but makes no comment – I can see the surprise in her eyes, those sparkling hazel eyes. My cock stiffens, pinpricked by the tightly laced leather sheath, balls separated by a web of buckled straps. Carolyn takes hold of my leash and forces me into a darkened corner where, to my delight, she presses her lips to mine, tongue working its slithery way into my mouth. A hand drops to my jock, squeezes. I groan, opening my legs to let her grab a feel of my sturdy cock, heavy balls, the pouched, strapped, sequestered equipment.

She is wearing a white blouse, pure silk, beneath which a lacy white bra struggles to hold captive a pair of beautifully orbed breasts with jutting, pink, proud nipples. I slide my hand under the short black skirt, feel suspender straps, sheer stockings, tiny white lace panties. Tugging them aside, I finger a hairless, cleanly shaved slit, already oozing with fuck juice. Carolyn is ready for my tongue, as I squat, push up the skirt, yank down the knickers, and bury my face into her warm moist cunt, licking all around it, chewing the labial lips, sucking on the tiny buttoned clit, listening to the sweet gasps, the whispered moans, feeling Carolyn come while I eat her out.

Pulling her panties back up, smoothing her skirt, she slides down my jock, unlaces the sheath, squats and gobbles my phallus straight to the back of her mouth, bobbing her head back and forth, slowly, then faster, creating a steady, unhurried rhythm. I don't take long to climax, and jet streams of sticky white jism along her tongue, into her throat. She sucks me dry.

After the club shuts, we take a taxi back to her palatial home. While I drink coffee, relaxing on the sofa, Carolyn disappears into the bedroom, 'to make myself comfortable'. She returns, and what a return: shiny black rubber, polished and buffed, coats her arms in opera-gloved fragility. The playsuit is partially open, unzipped to reveal a cleavage to die for. Long, spike-heeled boots make her appear taller, able to loom over me.

She orders me to undress, 'Remove everything.' Who am I to disobey? Once I am naked, Carolyn commands me to lie on the plush beige carpet. My cock stands proud and upright, drops of opaque fluid trickling from the tiny glans slit. She stands over me, directly in line with my hard-on. I shudder as she straddles me, impaling herself upon my rod, starting the ride, moving up and down, bouncing on my balls, cunt muscles gripping my shaft, dismounting before I can spunk. Then I am led through the lounge, to the kitchen, through a door and down some dark steps into a cellar. Carolyn clicks a switch to illuminate a low wattage bulb, to reveal not what I had expected, a room full of junk, but a carefully prepared dungeon, with frames and benches, chains and pulleys, racks and hooks for dildos, vibrators, canes. There are whips, paddles, riding crops, a myriad of toys and straps and leather.

Before I can take everything in, I am strapped, face forward, to a cross-frame, an 'X' of some dark polished wood, ball gagged, and whipped, the cat-o'-nine-tails striking its thin, painful lashes across my delicate flesh. I want to scream, but can't, not even able to sigh as Carolyn straps on a black rubber dildo, greases it up, and slides into me, fucking my ass as I should like to fuck her, hard and fast, without mercy, for her own pleasure, not mine, although I am getting pleasure; I love being fucked in the rear, usually by a hard-cocked stud, some guy I'll pick up in the club or through a variety of means. This time, it is Carolyn screwing me.

* * *

I am writing in response to your ad in *Private Eye* a couple of weeks ago. I lost the copy for a while, sorry for the lateness of this letter. I hope my handwriting is not too difficult, I usually write whilst at sea or in the cab of my van, so the delights of word processors, etc. are lost to me. I usually exchange sexual fantasies/stories with others (females) via an erotic correspondence club, so this is not as strange for me as it is for most people I assume – whilst it does seem strange to share it with another male for some reason.

I am not totally clear what exactly it is you require, as I have a lot of fantasies – do you just want the

63

most recurring one or my most vivid one currently or what? Anyway, this one I will write is the first one I had after my friend Jenny, an old hippie type, told me she would give me the 'gift' of lucid dreaming, it must have been some form of hypnosis, though she swore it was some sort of spell (she reckons she is a sorceress!) and ever since I've been so lucky – fantasies at night whenever I require! Enough rambling, now the Fantasy. Ahem!

In the fantasy I find myself in a bygone age, dressed in medieval attire. I am attending an important banquet, and take my seat at the long table between other men of importance, having first handed my sword to a servant, and pour myself some wine from a jug. The attractive middle-aged woman opposite me is obviously the powerful wife of the lord chieftain, and has two or three servants attending her, two small girls in their late twenties and a teenage lad.

Her eyes fix on me, and in no time we are engaged in flirting and suggestive word play, her fingers toying with her hair, her veil and the laces of her bodice, which retains quite a luxurious pair of breasts, honey-coloured skin shining wonderfully. Her eyes, dark and mysteriously sexual, stare into mine, my desire for her eating away at me, though I am aware of her partner just to her left engaged in earnest negotiation with his opposite number, a bishop, his attention to his wife's interest in me must not be aroused or I will be in big trouble!

Long, smouldering glances, each of us making subtle sexual play with pieces of food (a la Tom Jones, yes, huge cliché!) until I see her beckon two of her servants over, she whispers to each of them and they move off toward the end of the table out of view.

I am becoming more and more aroused by her actions, though my neighbouring diners are still unaware of what is going on. She reaches out to the large roast bird in the centre of the long table, and fastens her head around the large leg of the beast, caressing and pulling, trying to free it from the carcass. At the same time from beneath the table I feel my trousers being undone and lift the drapes to observe what is going on. The little servant girl is on her knees, impassive face looking at me as she frees my cock, which seems to leap into her hands. She motions with her finger to her lips as the sound of a throat being cleared opposite brings me back to a sitting position, my temptress opposite still grasping the leg of roast swan, caressing and pulling it as soft fingers enclose my hard shaft beneath the table and ease the foreskin back.

The 'queen' places her newly retrieved leg to her lips and licks at the fatty skin, seeming to enjoy it immensely. I watch entranced as a clever tongue dabs at the swollen helmet beneath the table, then swallows half of my length as her mistress does a similar thing with the roast joint, gradually with great and apparently much-practiced skill the servant girl brings me to orgasm, whilst I watch her mistress's visual simulation of oral stimulation with the piece of swan, seeming to be suppressing a mounting orgasm herself to judge from her flushed colour and politely heaving bosom. I feel the hand that is cradling my balls let go for a minute, then the hard points of two small ripe breasts press against my leg and the extra stimulation drives me over the edge, every effort heroically made to keep silent as a wave of euphoria almost overwhelms me and I feel myself emptying, being expertly milked of all my seed.

Opposite me my hostess is wide-eyed, shuddering and coughing, pretending to choke it seems as she grips the arms of her chair and her maid slaps her back. I raise the drapes once more, the girl is wiping her mouth and commences pushing her small, large-nippled breasts back into her bodice, a faint smile on her lips as I watch her slide away, accompanied by another body from the opposite side of the table. I rise to my seat once more, my act of tying my boot complete, and observe the lovely little maid and the teenage boy back at their mistress's side and receiving a small coin each. The 'queen' gives me a long smouldering glance and rises to leave.

I look over at the chieftain, his strange gaze has fixed upon me, and I look for my swordbelt. This is where it all usually ends – which is great as he is a big bastard and I have no desire to get involved in vividly real disemboweling!

There, I hope that didn't frighten your horses/budgie/fishtank too much, I can write it better if you like. Now, any chance of a freebie book? (Yes, I'm a cheapskate scrounger but a deal's a deal!)

P.S. Sorry about scruffy writing, paper, missing sides, everything really. I'll get my coat then . . .

* * *

My fantasy: ladies' teeth. My fantasy stories: Meet Bill Dennington the timid accountant who designs brassieres in his spare time, and a host of huge busty ladies including a Hollywood starlet with an unbelievable chest. Meet naughty dentists, even naughtier nurses and the folk singer who did her act with a topless gown and only a guitar for cover, and took repeated bows.

THE QUESTIONNAIRE

Are you: heterosexual? Yes.

What, if anything, do you find offensive? Please list things – objects, actions or even attitudes – which are to do with sex or which are often associated with sex and which offend you. In photographs, on television or in films: violence, coercion, sex/love as a tradeable commodity in relationships.

In real life: using power/status/influence in order to obtain sex.

Name – supplied; *address* – supplied. *Your occupation:* long-term illness.

About your sexual fantasies. (Definition: What you think about when you think about sex in such a way that you become sexually aroused) How often, on average, do you have sexual fantasies? Several times a day.

Do your fantasies tend to have recurring themes or subjects? Yes. *If there are recurring themes or subjects, what are they?* Dominant/assertive women. Group sex/parties, sex in public places or outdoors.

Do you have a current favourite fantasy, or a fantasy that you enjoy more than most? I'm a member of an adult penfriend club and regularly exchange really explicit fantasies with (at present) four very horny women. I'd be glad to let you have details.

About your sexuality: Think back to when you were discovering your sexuality, your sexual orientation, and the sexual themes that are now part of your personality. What did you find erotic in those days? What things (for instance films, or books, or items of clothing) or people or experiences were a turn-on?

- Very late developer – no interest at all until 27. I thought I was possibly totally asexual.
- At present prefer long sessions of oral sex and mutual masturbation. Cannot resist women who do not wear perfume.

What things or people or experiences are particular turn-ons now?

- In real life, more than anything, honesty.
- But also stripping/touching games and situations.
- Obviously, my randy penfriends and the occasional telephone sex session.

Describe – in detail, don't be shy – the best sex you've ever had (so far!). As before, continue on a separate sheet if you prefer.

- Wendy – a nurse, of course. Very open and upfront. Within minutes we were shagging. Only two house rules when visiting: no clothes and constant bodily contact – all my erections to be demolished by her body in the kinkiest ways possible.

What would improve your sex life?

- Finding a regular partner or a group of swingers. I don't have any mental hang-ups or physical problems – in fact, I'm getting randier by the day.

* * *

In the pub one night, I got talking to a man who told me about a practice he assured me was known as 'dogging'. When I asked him to explain further he said that there was a wood on the edge of town couples would go to to have sex in their cars while people watched. This idea appealed to me strongly, and since that drink I've been thinking about how my girlfriend Liz would react if I mentioned it casually. Here's the fantasy:

When I mention my conversation to Liz, she admits that the thought of fucking in such a public spot was something she had often fantasised about. It would give her another chance to flaunt her body and take her exhibitionism to the next level, but in what she considered was a relatively safe environment. A couple of nights later, we drive up to that spot to see if what I been told was true.

When we get there, we can't believe what we see. A rusty white van is parked up, of the kind painters and decorators often use, with about three or four men gathered round the back. After a couple of moment's speculation about what might be going on in the van, Liz and I work up the courage to go quietly out of the car and join the crowd. The back doors of the van are thrown open and there, amid a litter of paint pots and rags which give off a strong scent of turpentine, we can see a bare-breasted blonde straddling a man's body, facing my feet. She is bouncing up and down and playing with her nipples. Every time she pulls herself up off him, I can see that she must be sliding down on a good nine inches of solid cock. Although she must be completely aware of the audience's presence she is completely oblivious to it.

This is all the encouragement Liz needs. We get in the car and drive home so fast I'm amazed I don't get clocked by a speed camera. We're so turned on, Liz by the idea of disporting herself in the way the blonde had been, that we spend the rest of the night fucking. As I pound into Liz's wet quim, my head is full of the vision of that big, blue-veined cock sliding in and out of that blonde's juiced-up cunt. Liz and I talk it over the following morning, and decide that although we're not prepared to go quite as far as the couple we had seen – after all, anyone could have reached into the back of that van and joined in the action – we really want to give it a go. A week later, we drive up to the dogging spot. The clearing where we had seen the white van is empty, so we park there, climb on to the back seat and get down to the sort of petting that is usually indulged in by young couples who don't have a private space of their own where they can fuck.

I can feel Liz's heart pounding in her chest as I pull her top up and unclip the fastening of her bra, and I know she is as nervous as I am. I suckle on her nipple as she unbuttons the fly of my jeans. I'm always 'going commando', so the next thing I feel is her warm hand on my rapidly hardening cock. She wanks me expertly with one hand, cupping my balls and squeezing them with the other, while my mouth feasts on her tits. Suddenly, we become aware of shadows against the car window, and know that our audience has arrived. Hoping we have been joined by a keen voyeur or two, rather than a couple of members of the local constabulary, I push Liz down so that she is lying on the seat, and pull her knickers off. Even though there is plenty of condensation on the windows, I'm sure whoever is watching is getting a good view of her creamy pussy as she raises her bum to let me undress her more easily. I finger her for a moment or two, hearing the urgent groans which always let me know she's ready to feel my cock inside her, and then I kneel over her, put the head of my glans to her moist entrance, and slide home. The force of our fucking makes the car rock on its axles, and know that even if people cannot see what we are doing, the noise would be a giveaway. Liz is begging me to fuck her harder, and I am happy to oblige, as my balls grow tight and I know I am about to shoot my lot inside her. Her semi-clad body stiffens beneath me and then stills, and I know she has peaked, my own climax following only moments behind.

When we have recovered and dressed, I rub the steam from the window and look out to see our audience has gone. When we get home and out of the car, I see that there are long streaks of what can only be dried come on both rear doors, proving that at least two people had both been wanking while they watched us fuck. I imagine that we have returned there a few times, and the number of people watching us grows. We even begin to fuck with the doors open, or even getting out of the car. I love the idea of pressing Liz up against the bonnet while I pump my cock into her from behind, our audience cheering us on, urging me to do it whatever way takes my fancy.

* * *

I'm what you'd call a breast man, but with me, the fetish goes further than just admiring a nice pair of tits in the street, or spending a long time licking and sucking my wife's glorious nipples. For as long as I can remember, I have had the urge to taste a woman's breast milk. Nothing would give me greater pleasure than to suckle my wife and taste her milk, but Collette and I have decided not to have children, and so it seemed that my fantasy was destined to stay just that.

Three months ago, Collette's sister, Yolanda, gave birth to a baby son, and it's given my fantasy new impetus. Often, when I'm fucking Collette,

I'll imagine that I am with Yolanda, fondling her breasts, which I know are heavy and swollen with milk. I had thought that Collette might have mixed feelings at seeing her sister achieve something she never would, but she's pleased for her, spending a lot of time babysitting her little nephew and buying him presents. Collette told Yolanda that if there was ever anything she needed, we would be more than happy to oblige. Yolanda's husband, Jacob, is a bit of a ne'er-do-well, and while he's managed to get in a certain amount of time with his new son, he soon left Yolanda on her own again. That's when she started to invite us round more frequently, because Collette loves spending time with the baby. It's an arrangement that seems to suit us all.

I imagine, however, that Yolanda rings up in panic as the washing machine has broken down, and she doesn't know what to do. There's water all over the place she says, and she can't really struggle with a load of dirty washing and the baby. As I used to be a plumber by trade (and no, I never got a come-on from a randy housewife!) I tell Yolanda to sit tight and I'll be round to take a look at it. Yolanda greets me at the door of her flat. She apologises for the fact that she looks a mess, but I barely notice her unbrushed hair and the dark circles that ring her eyes. I can't tear my eyes from her chest. She's wearing a navy shirt, and it's obvious that her breast milk has gone through her bra, and is soaking the cotton even darker. Even though this is my wife's sister, I can feel my cock stirring in my overalls as my fantasies come flooding back. The washing machine is easy to fix – it was a problem with the door seal that only took me minutes to sort out. By the time I've finished and we've mopped the soapy water from the kitchen floor, I'm dying for a drink. Yolanda offers me a cup of tea and I accept, even though I had another kind of drink in mind, as I'm sure you can imagine.

Yolanda and I sit in the lounge, drinking our tea, and then she drops the bombshell. She tells me that since she's had the baby, as far as Jacob is concerned, she has completely lost her sex appeal. She claims he can hardly bear to touch her, and she's sure he finds her ugly, with her stretchmarked stomach and her swollen, leaking tits. I tell her she's talking rubbish; as far as I'm concerned, I have never seen her look so beautiful, and as for her breasts . . . Despite myself, I begin to spill my secret: the fact that I have always wanted to drink breast milk. I would never do anything to hurt Collette, I swear, and yet, looking at Yolanda, with her big tits so obviously full of milk, I'm seized with the overwhelming urge to sink to the floor and bury my face in that wonderful, ripe cleavage.

'Do it,' Yolanda urges. 'Please Richard, do it. The baby's been fed and I've got more than enough to spare.' As she speaks, she's pulling her T-shirt over her head. Her breasts are cradled in a white cotton nursing bra, the material wet through where it presses against her dark, stiff nipples. As she unhooks the catch of her bra and lets her tits fall free, I know my ultimate desire is about to be realised. I race over to the settee where she is sitting and rest my head on her breast. She strokes my wiry hair as my lips clamp hold of her rubbery nipple and begin to suck. Instantly, my mouth is filled with rich, sweet-tasting milk, and I gulp it down like a thirsty man who's found an oasis in the desert. My hand caresses the soft, cushiony flesh of her other breast, and as I look up briefly I can see that her eyes are half-closed and she seems lost in a world of her own sensual ecstasy. I know I shouldn't do what I do next but I can't help myself. The skirt she's wearing is rucked up, and I slip my hand under it, stroking the soft flesh of her thighs. She makes no move to stop me and as my fingers moved higher, they touch the fabric of her panties. They're very wet, as her bra had been, and I know then that she's taking a deeply sexual pleasure in what I'm doing to her.

By now, my cock's desperate for relief, and Yolanda makes no protest as my lips finally release their grip on her nipple and I lay her back on the settee. I quickly strip off my overalls, before pulling down her panties and spreading her legs wide. Her crease is shining with her juices, the lips peeling apart easily to give me access to her cunt. With one firm thrust I'm inside her. She groans in pleasure as my shaft lodges between her velvet walls. I pause for a moment, savouring the sensation, before I begin to fuck her steadily. Within moments she's coming, her pussy spasming around my cock, and I wonder how her husband can be so stupid as not to appreciate what a beautiful, sexy woman he has. That's my last coherent thought before my own orgasm hits and I pump my load inside her. In my fantasy, Yolanda and I promise each other that that afternoon will be a one-off. However, I can't deny that I'd love a suckle from those beautiful tits, and can't help but wonder if they taste as good as they look.

*   *   *

Whether it's submissive or not I don't know, but I've always had a thing about watching my girlfriend – and I've always thought about it, with all of them – with another man or other men. Perhaps I just like the idea of her being a dirty little slut, perhaps I just like to watch sex (let's face it, you can't usually see much of it when it's you doing it). Maybe it's because

I'm fascinated by the strength of feeling it would arouse. Anyway, here's a story about what I like to imagine!

It would never have happened if Peggy and I hadn't had that row. The silly thing is that I can't remember what it was about. Something to do with me not paying her enough attention, I think. Anyway, it was the culmination of a series of rows we had been having. Money was tight as I was on half-time, our sex life was almost nonexistent, which gave us plenty of things to fight about. I do recall that she said something to the effect that if she couldn't get it from me she was going to get it somewhere else. I said that was fine by me. I thought it was just one of those things that get said in the heat of the moment. I never thought she was serious.

She grabbed her coat, her bag and her key, said she was off out. I thought she was going to walk round the block, to clear her head and cool down, and so I simply shrugged and went back to the TV programme I had been trying to watch. When she hadn't come back an hour later, I started to get a bit concerned, but I assumed she'd gone round to a mate's house. I went to bed around midnight, and was woken at four in the morning by Peggy staggering into the bedroom, obviously trying, poorly, not to make any noise. I switched the light on, and immediately realised she had been up to something: her tights were laddered, her hair was a mess and her make-up was smeared around her face, and she had a self-satisfied smirk on her face. 'Where have you been till now?' I asked, still half-asleep.

'Doing what I said I'd do,' she replied. 'I told you I'd go out and get sex somewhere else, and I did.' My initial reaction was one of disbelief, anger and a strange excitement.

'Yeah, right,' I retorted.

'Don't you believe me, Mike?' she said. 'Do you want me to give you the details? Well, I picked him up in the pub round the corner, he was nineteen years old and he had an eight-inch cock that was so thick I could hardly get my mouth round it.' Strangely, I was as hard as a rock under the sheets; jealous, hurt, and wanting Peggy to tell me more. She took off her top and skirt and flung them to the floor. Even in the dim light from the bedside lamp I thought I could see a telltale wet patch in the front of her knickers. 'When I left here, all I knew was that I was determined to get laid, and I thought the best place to go was the pub,' Peggy said. 'I saw him drinking at the bar with his mates. He was the best-looking one of the lot. He was big-built, with blond hair cut really short and a big Celtic tattoo running round his biceps. He looked like the sort who'd be up for a quick fuck with no finesse, so I just went up and started giving him the come-on.'

I know what that involves. When Peggy and I first met she did exactly the same thing: came up to me when I was in a crowd of blokes and undid just enough buttons on her blouse that I could see her bra and the tits that were doing their best to burst out of it. I couldn't see how any man could resist her if she was determined to snare him, and it sounded like the unknown young stud had not put up too much of a fight. 'He didn't waste any time once he realised I was up for it,' she said. 'Within a few minutes we were snogging at the bar. He had his tongue right down my throat and his hand up my top, mauling my tits through my bra. He had really rough calluses like he worked on a building site or something and I knew he'd want it hard and fast when we got to fucking.

'As we kissed, he encouraged me to feel the bulge in his jeans. As soon as I touched it, I realised it was big – a lot bigger than yours, James – and the thought of all that meaty, firm cock flesh, combined with the way he was fondling my tits, was getting me really wet. I wanted him now, and he asked if we were off to my place or his, the cocky sod. I said it would have to be his because my inadequate wimp of a boyfriend was sulking at home, and while I wanted him to know a real man had fucked me, I didn't want to give him the satisfaction of watching.'

The gratuitous insults she was throwing coupled with the image she was painting of the uncouth builder groping her so openly in front of his mates was fuelling my erection, and I couldn't resist slipping a hand down under the duvet to tug at my stiff length. 'As we were leaving,' Peggy continued, 'his friends shouted, "See you later, Horse." Horse told me his name was Pete, and so I asked – stupidly perhaps – why his mates called him Horse. Bold as brass, he said it was because they all knew he was hung like one. He lived in this really grotty bedsit over a chippy. When you walked in there, the smell of frying fat and fish struck you immediately. He said he was used to it but, to me, it just added to the sleaziness of what I was doing. He told me to strip, just like that, and to lie on the bed with my legs spread while he undressed, so he could look at my cunt while he was doing it.' Now sex between Peggy and me might not be all that frequent, but when it happens I always make the effort to spend a long time kissing her, touching her and making sure she's nice and ready for me by the time I enter her. It seemed like foreplay was a foreign concept to her new conquest, but she said she found his crude language and direct approach a turn-on. 'I mean, sometimes you can be too much of a gentleman, James,' she said. 'I won't break if you slam your cock into me really hard, you know.

Anyway, Horse said that if I wanted to be wet for him, then I should play with myself. And I did: I lay there on the unmade bed in that smelly little room and frigged my clit while he took his clothes off. When his pants came down, it was obvious his cock was everything I'd been promised and more. It was so long and thick, it makes yours look like a little boy's prick in comparison.

'I was expecting Horse to just leap on me and start fucking me but, to my surprise, he said, "I want to do something to you that will make sure your boyfriend knows you've been with someone else." And do you know what he did? This . . .' As Peggy spoke, she was pulling down her knickers. The sight that greeted me as she did so caused the breath to catch in my throat. When I'd seen her naked earlier that morning, her mound had been crowned with its big, thick gauze of black curls. Now, all that had gone, leaving pink, shiny bare skin. This young stud had left his proprietorial mark by shaving my girl-friend's cunt. My hand began to move faster on my cock as I gawped at her. 'He went into his bathroom and came back with a can of shaving foam and a razor. Just like that, he squirted the foam over my pussy, and began to hack away at my pubes. As the lather and hair came away, I could see my naked skin beneath it, all pink and vulnerable. He was pulling my lips around and making sure he got into all the nooks and crannies, and the really impersonal way he was touching me was getting me horny. By the time he'd finished, my cunt was all smooth and shiny, like a pool ball, and I was just desperate to be fucked. I pulled him on top of me, guiding his cock to my aching hole. I could really feel the difference between you and him as his big, meaty shaft slid right up into me, and the scratch of his pubes against my newly shaved skin was like nothing I'd known before. I felt so sensitive, and even though he was just concentrating on his own pleasure as he thrust into me, I was coming off all over his cock. Then he spunked into me, climbed off and that was it. Not even a kiss or a word to say if he'd enjoyed it. I felt used and slutty and it was absolutely fantastic.'

By now, my own orgasm seemed inevitable, and I pulled back the duvet to reveal my own cock, its head shiny with pre-come. Peggy told me she couldn't remember the last time she'd seen it so big, even though she said it was still nothing in comparison to Horse's massive member. I begged her to fuck me, but she said she was too sore from the pounding Horse had given her denuded cunt. She wanked me off until I shot my load, my come flying into the air to land on my own stomach. The following morning, however, I did get to screw her beautiful shaved pussy. If she were to agree to remain shaved, on condition that I let her go back and sample Horse's huge cock again. I could live with that!

* * *

I'm not much of a football fan but I could really handle jumping into the communal steam bath in the dressing room with Fulham Ladies'. They're the premier UK women's soccer club, in which America leads the field. Seeing that satiny football gear on women gives it a whole new slant to me: seeing a couple of shaved, shapely legs sticking out from the flimsy material, seeing women run with such determination. I get the whole perky, upskirt thing about tennis players, of course, but I prefer my women a bit older, twenties or so, so maybe football's a new sport to watch in an erotic light! Anyway, I wouldn't mind easing their pressures, and guessing which one was going to drop the soap next.

* * *

Since my wife and I moved to California to live and work, we have discovered a whole new side to our sexuality that we never knew existed. People are far more open about sex here than they are in Britain, and once they discover that you have a particular kink, they are only too happy to help you indulge.

Like a lot of couples who have been married for a while, Linda and I had tried a few things to try to recapture the excitement of our early days together. She had dressed in sexy underwear and rubber, I had spanked her on occasions, and we had even tried making love outdoors on the lawn on hot summer evenings, knowing that there was a chance our neighbours might see what we were doing. However, none of these really gave us the added spice we were looking for, and it was when we began to experiment with watersports that we really found our niche. Linda has a mildly submissive side to her nature, but she doesn't like pain, which is why being spanked did very little for her. It was only one evening when, in a moment of drunken bravado, I ordered her to strip off and lie down in the bath, then pissed on her that she began to get very excited. By the time I had soaked her body head to foot in a hot, golden stream of urine, she was more turned on than I could remember, and the fuck that followed was mindblowing.

I have made some good friends at work, and happened to mention to one of them, Kurt, that Linda and I had discovered a love for pissing. He told me that this was one of his own personal turn-ons, and that he had once been to what was called a 'piss party', where like-minded people got to play all sorts of wet games. I mentioned this to Linda, and she suggested that we should hold our own party, and invite Kurt and a couple of others to join in. Needless to say, Kurt was delighted by our invitation, and the following Saturday, he arrived at our house at seven o'clock prompt, along with friends, Matthew and Glenn. Linda had provided drinks and some food – with the emphasis, of course, on the drinks – and we sat in our lounge, chatting, listening to music while we men downed glass after glass of lager. The knowledge of what was to come added a strong edge of sexual tension to our conversation, and I found myself getting hard at the thought of these strangers pissing on Linda's lovely body. At last, it was time to go upstairs. Linda showed some reluctance to take things further. To encourage her I grabbed her by the arm and hauled her forcefully. I knew this was her submissive streak coming to the fore, and the more she protested, the more excited she was getting as I asserted my dominance over her. In the bathroom, I ordered her to take off the beaded cocktail dress she was wearing. What she had on beneath it could not have been more seductive: her bra and matching panties were of nylon, and did nothing to conceal her long and luxuriant blonde pubic bush. Lace hold-up stockings completed the outfit. As she shook her hair from its clip to let it tumble over her shoulders, we four men quickly undressed, revealing four penises in varying stages of erectness in tribute to my wife's beauty.

She got into the bath without undressing further, and lay down. I looked at our guests, inviting one of them to go first. Instead, the three stepped into the bath together, and positioned themselves around

Linda's body – Kurt at her head, Glenn by her midriff and Matt at her feet. Then, as if at some signal they had prearranged between them, they began to piss. Three powerful jets of liquid hit Linda simultaneously, gushing over her face and down her body, soaking the flimsy underwear she wore and sending it almost transparent. Linda lay back, eyes half-closed and mouth open, lost in her own private world, and when Kurt directed his stream between her red-glossed lips, she did not even flinch, but drank it down with relish.

At last, the three of them finished, and looked to me to conclude proceedings. I asked them to strip her completely, and they complied eagerly, rolling down her sodden stockings and peeling off her bra and knickers. I told Linda to open her legs wide, and as she did we could all clearly see that her cunt was not only wet with piss but with the glistening evidence of her arousal. I straddled her supine body and she moaned in anticipation, begging me to piss in her face and over her big tits and pussy. I let fly, aiming a torrent of piss directly at her exposed sex and playing it over her swollen clit. She writhed in the bath, pulling at her own nipples in appreciation of the sheer erotic degradation I was putting her through. I have never seen Linda so aroused as she was that night, and my three American friends were amply rewarded by her for their prowess – but that's a story for another time.

* * *

I'm pretty perverted, but not in an overly submissive or dominant way, particularly, and the few times I've tried to play a role as such with someone I haven't been able to keep a straight face! No, I crave a partner with whom I can share as equals all the filthy, messy goings-on I'd like to try. And there's nothing I'd want her to do which I wouldn't try myself. My partner Jane and I have experimented sexually since we first met, and I don't think there's much we haven't tried. But I haven't yet got around to mentioning a growing fascination with watersports, a fascination which I suppose arises because it seems so wetly intimate and, in a way, close. There's a game we could play a few times which would turn me – and, I'm sure, her – on incredibly because we could do it without anyone else knowing what we are up to. I think the conspiratorial quality would probably appeal to her.

If were going out for the evening, she could wear her sexiest underwear. Not only would this make her feel good, but it would be the ideal preparation for what is to come. Jane would wear a black satin corset, which I would lace very tightly indeed for her. By the time I had finished, her waist would be much narrower than normal, and her already very large breasts would be emphasised even further. Then she would fasten suspenders to the straps which hang down from the corset, and wear my favourite floor-length red velvet dress over the top. No knickers!

Then the fun begins. I will make sure that before Jane and I have left the house, she has drunk an entire bottle of mineral water, and for the rest of the evening, wherever we are, I will keep providing her with more drinks at regular intervals. Of course, you can imagine the effect all this liquid begins to have, and soon she is becoming anxious to use the toilet. However, as she well knows, that is most definitely not allowed. The tight corset is very restrictive, and it causes an extra pressure on her bladder. If we have gone to see a play or a concert, she'd find it almost impossible to sit still in her seat, and this would become more of an ordeal as the evening progresses. If we are at a dinner party or a social function, it would be easier for her to get up and walk about, though sure she must be drawing attention to herself as she tries to cross her legs discreetly to fight the overwhelming urge to pee. By the end of the evening, she's finding it almost impossible to hold on any longer. I can see exactly how much discomfort she is in as she bites her lip in the back of the taxi and presses her hand between her legs. She's afraid she'll disgrace herself in the back of the taxi. When we get home, her first instinct is to dive for the toilet, but I tell her that that's not how this game is going to be played. By now, she's taking the tiniest of steps because she knows that strenuous movement will cause her pee to start uncontrollably leaking out, or even scared to move at all. I help her out of her dress, but not corset or the stockings. Then I'd tell her to step into the bath. Just climbing over the edge of the bath would be tortuous and she might even start to wee in the process.

I look at Jane as she stands there, very much turned on by seeing her in this state. She begs me to finally let her pee, but I've got one last trick up my sleeve. I tell her she can't until she has made herself come. Her clitoris would be particularly sensitive by now, and her bladder swollen and distended. And to reach between her legs and begin to finger herself on top of such tension would be an additional stimulation that is too much. Unable to control herself, she begins to pee, the golden liquid trickling down over her hand as she rubs at her pussy like a woman possessed. I imagine that by the time she has finished, her thighs and the tops of her stockings are a mixture of urine and love juice. Humiliation shines in her eyes. Stripping off as I watch her, I turn her over and enter her roughly from behind. Just before I come, I pull out and spray my semen over her globed ass-cheeks, watching it slide down to mix with her own fluids. At last, I begin to unlace the corset as the tension ebbs away and we relax. As I said, what appeals to me about this is that no one would work out what Jane and I are doing, or why she looks so flushed and excited when we're out for the evening. I think it's the sense of conspiracy behind the humiliation that appeals to me about this idea.

* * *

My girlfriend, who is eighteen, and I were out shopping a couple of Saturdays ago. It was a hot day, and Zoe had been swigging from a big bottle of water as we walked around the shops. Suddenly, she told me that she needed to use the loo. We were in a large department store at the time, so she went to find the ladies' toilets, only to discover that they were out of order. Zoe said it didn't matter, as she could hold on until we got home. We went in two or three more shops, none of which had a toilet, and by this time it was getting obvious that Zoe needed to go quite badly. She was jogging from foot to foot, or standing cross-legged, obviously trying to lessen the pressure on her bladder. During the bus ride home, which took nearly twice as long as it should have due to roadworks holding up the traffic, she kept her legs tightly crossed and fidgeted, having again dismissed the suggestion that she should look for a loo before we got on the bus. By now, part of me was beginning to hope that she would lose the struggle to hold on to her bladder and would wet herself where she was sitting. The thought of that was exciting enough to get my cock twitching in my underpants. I had never realised that this was something I wanted, but I guess it was.

When we finally got home, she said, 'That's it, I have to go to the loo. I just can't wait any longer.' However, I did my best to persuade her to hang on just a little longer. I confessed to her that I was incredibly turned on by the obvious predicament she was in, and that one of my long-standing fantasies was to fuck a girl who was desperately in need of a piss. She looked a bit shocked at this, but I sensed that deep down the thought was turning her on too.

We hurried up to the bedroom, where Zoe pulled the duvet off the bed and put a couple of towels down to soak up the flow. Then we both were naked from the waist down, and we got on the bed. We were soon sharing deep kisses while I cupped her firm tits through her top. I moved my hand down so I could feel the gorgeous shape of her tummy, which was swollen and bloated with her pee. At the feel of this gentle pressure on her bladder, she groaned, and I saw a little gush spurt out on to the towel beneath her.

Thrusting a hand between her thighs, I stroked her clit, which was sticking out stiffly from its hood, indicating just how aroused she was. As I continued to massage her tummy and wank her at the same time, I could see she was torn between excitement and embarrassment, wetting herself while I played with her. By now, my cock was begging for its own release, and I resisted the growing temptation to wank it. I wanted to come in Zoe's hot, tight cunt, and I knew the time was approaching when she would finally give me permission to enter her. By now, her pee was a steady trickle she was no longer making any attempt to hide. Her eyes were closed as she moved closer to release. At last, she finally let go and began to urinate. Her pee streamed over my hand, she was getting me so excited that I just pushed her legs wide apart, thrust my cock into her incredible pussy and fucked her while the last of her pee dribbled on to my balls.

* * *

My two fetishes are PVC and peeing. I'd like to tell you about the ways in which I fantasise about combining the two. I first discovered these were my turn-ons when I went to university. Until then, I had been sheltered from the kinkier byways of sex. I was no virgin – I lost that on my seventeenth birthday to a girl I'd been seeing for a year, but found sex to be a disappointing experience and I couldn't see why people made so much fuss. Then I discovered the fetish scene through magazines – I was surprised that they turned me on so much as they weren't explicit as such, but suffused with so much sexuality that they were hornier than looking at a straightforward porn mag that left nothing to the imagination. Then I met Patricia, who was in her final year, and knew a hell of a lot more about sex than I did. We had tried a limited amount of sexy underwear that had consisted of stockings, suspenders and a G-string, and while it excited me, it was obvious to me that they just pointed the way to more elaborate and pervy clothing. We broke up after a couple of terms, amicably – just having drifted apart over the long summer holiday. I don't know where she is now, but I still fantasise about her. I suppose I regret not having broached the issue of fetishism with her as she was one of the most attractive and responsive girls I've been with and, with the confidence that I have now, I'd predict that she'd have been well up for it.

So I imagine I'm back at uni. She's so much more experienced than me and I have to even the score somehow, show her something that she doesn't know about yet. So I take her to a fetish clothing shop in West London, because I want her to dress up for sex. To see her in something more suited to my fetish. I don't know what I'm expecting myself when we set out shopping. It looks, on the outside, like a light industrial unit, and inside it smells like one too, with all the rubber hanging loosely on the racks and the fluid used to shine it up. She runs her hand tentatively over a little black dress, and says she can't believe that people get such a buzz from wrapping themselves in the cold, clammy stuff. However, I have something slightly different in mind for her. I pick out a peephole PVC bra, matching crotchless knickers, and a PVC macintosh which she could go out in without anyone turning a hair. That of course is exactly what I intend her to do.

She steps into the little cubicle and strips off. The bra and knickers look as though they have been made for her, and while they look sleazy, combined with the black hold-up stockings she's wearing, they do not look cheap, as a skimpy nylon set from a more usual sex shop would do. She puts the mac on over the top and does a twirl, delighting me, and her with her new reflection in the mirror. When she goes to take it off before I pay for it, I shake my head. 'Keep it on,' I say, 'you're going home, like that.' She stares at me, open-mouthed, as the shop assistant cheerfully bundles the clothes she has been wearing into a carrier bag. She wonders what sort of a game I'm playing, but knows that she has no choice but to go along with it.

We step out into the sunshine, her looking some-what overdressed in the shiny black mac and wondering what people would say if they knew how little she has on underneath it. It's a warm day, and she's soon sweating beneath the heavy PVC. The rough lining is also stimulating her exposed nipples, and she finds herself beginning to get strangely turned on – as turned on as I am. As we take the tube back to the university, I take the opportunity to fondle her barely clad bum through the mac. I press up against her so that she can feel the hefty bulge in my jeans and knows that I, too, am turned on by the situation. I think for a moment of ordering her to open the mac and flash her nipples and lightly trimmed mound at our fellow commuters. My cock twitches as I realise how much I would enjoy making her do that.

However, the only things I have on my mind now are sex and pee. I picture us in my old study-bedroom. My hands dart up underneath the hem of her mac, searching out her slippery, moist cunt. The room is small, and the smell of the PVC, perspiration and my musky arousal hangs heavy. She groans as my fingers part the lips of her quim, and she strokes and squeezes her own breasts through the mac, feeling her nipples harden as they rub against the coarse lining material. That is when she becomes aware of another sensation, as my clever fingers stroke her towards a climax. Suddenly, she doesn't just want to come, she wants to pee as well. She pulls away from me and announces she needs the toilet.

'No, you don't,' I reply, 'not when you've got your mac. Why not take it off?' She does as I ask, unbuttoning it and laying it on the floor beneath us, telling me her need to pee is becoming unbearable, and wondering still whether I expect her to dart, in her skimpy kinky underwear, to the communal bath-room. The hall of residence in which I'm living is single-sex, and she wonders how the other residents would react if they saw her dashing for the loo in her revealing PVC bra and pants, her pouting nipples and wet cunny clearly on display. She endeavours to twist from my embrace and tells me that if I don't let her go that instance, she's going to wet herself. 'Then do it,' I say. 'Wet yourself.'

Before she can protest, my hand presses against her lovely stomach, putting a pressure on her bladder she's unable to fight. I imagine her groan as she feels the moisture of her urine leak out of her to spatter on her mac. And then the floodgates open, she's wetting herself without thought of the consequences, feeling the relief as her bladder empties into a pool on the shiny mac. My erection is threatening to burst the zip of my jeans. I push her down so we're lying in the pool of her own making, and then we have hot, frantic sex on the pee-soaked mac, my cock bigger and harder than I ever remember it as it thrusts up into her wet cunt. The smell of PVC coupled with her urine is almost overpowering, but it simply spurs her on to another shattering orgasm. I imagine, in return for all the gymnastics she taught me, that I could have introduced Patricia to another rewarding dimension of sex, and I'm sorry that at the time I didn't have the guts to try – at least with the PVC stuff!

* * *

My wife Angie once confessed to me that her deepest fantasy was to take part in a gang-bang. She said she was incredibly turned on by the thought of being used by at least four men, but we never could find a way of turning this fantasy into reality, as it's hardly the sort of thing we could ask our close friends to join in, and we didn't like the idea of contact magazines. In the end, we decided to keep it as just that, a fantasy, since it seemed like the reality would probably get messed up somehow if we tried.

I imagine I've got a job as the head waiter in a restaurant which has a high turnover of casual staff. There are always lots of students looking for part-time work to supplement their loans, and when I mentioned this to Angie it plants the seed of an idea in our heads. We're both in our late thirties, and the thought of being shagged senseless by a group of fit young men aged about nineteen or twenty really appeals to her, so she asks me to suggest it to the ones I thought most likely to go for it. I feel a bit stupid trying to recruit other men to have sex with my wife. At first, they think I'm joking, or some kind of inadequate wimp who can't satisfy a woman, but when they realise I'm serious, and that I'm giving them carte blanche to do whatever they want to her, I soon find four who agree.

So it is that, one Friday night after the restaurant shuts, I find myself taking Jimmy, Dan, Geoff and Rick back to our flat, where Angie was waiting. Angie has dressed for the part in the most sluttish outfit she possesses. She's wearing a see-through cream blouse over a black uplift bra, a short, tight black miniskirt, stockings, suspenders and stiletto-heeled court shoes. She is wearing a lot more make-up than she normally would, and her blonde hair looks tousled and tangled, as though she's just got out of bed. As she has a great figure and just oozes sex when she is dressed this way, I could not see any of the lads failing to get turned on by her. She has laid on drinks and nibbles, and as she goes round with a tray, introducing herself to everyone, I'm gratified to see that Jimmy, who is rapidly becoming the natural ringleader of the group, is not shy in fondling her bum as she passes.

Once they're all sorted with glasses of beer and something to eat, I slip a tape into the video recorder for a bit of autosuggestion. It's one I had picked up on a trip to Amsterdam, and it is one of Angie's favourites. It features a woman being fucked by three men at the same time, and in the scene that's playing, she is squatting over a big black guy, sliding up and down on his cock, while one of his colleagues is shafting her asshole. Dan and Geoff watch the action on the TV screen open-mouthed, but Rick seems to have taken the hint. Rick starts kissing Angie and pawing her tits through her clothes, while Jimmy runs his hands up and down her thighs, pushing at her black skirt until it rides up and her stocking tops are clearly visible. Rick is hurriedly unbuttoning Angie's blouse as their tongues battle together, and Jimmy is pulling my wife's legs apart. As he does, the others – who are by now rapidly losing their inhibitions – and I are treated to the superb sight of Angie's cunt revealed through the split in the pair of crotchless knickers she was wearing. I have seen those knickers before, and I'd thought she might select them specifically for this evening.

Once Angie's blouse is off, Rick pays attention to her bra, not taking it off but pulling her big breasts free from the cups, leaving the cups and straps to frame and uplift them. She looks magnificently cheap sitting there with her clothes in disarray and her tits and pussy on display; I see Dan is stroking his cock through his trousers and my own erection is straining to be let free of my pants. I had not expected to be quite so turned on by the sight of these relative strangers toying with my wife but now it's happening, I can't get my cock out fast enough and Jimmy has undone Angie's skirt to encourage her to wriggle out of it, and now she's nestling on the settee between the two men in her tarty underwear. Rick is suckling one tit while his fingers twist the nipple of the other, and Jimmy is moving his hand between Angie's legs. I mute the volume on the video, so instead of the faked moaning of the actress as she comes, we're treated to the genuine, wet, squelching sound of Jimmy's fingers exploring the juicy folds of my wife's pussy.

'I want you to suck me off, you dirty slut,' Rick told my wife. I had let the lads know that using the crudest of language gets Angie really horny, and it is obvious from the way she hurries to free his manhood from his trousers that his words are having the desired effect. Erect, Rick's cock is no bigger than my own five and a half inches, but it looks very thick, with a bulbous head that my wife's lips are struggling to wrap themselves around. Meanwhile, Jimmy has stripped off completely. He, too, has an average-sized member, which he's bringing to full hardness with a few swift rubs. He urges Angie on to all fours so that she can keep on sucking Rick while he guides his cockhead through the slit in her knickers into her expectant pussy. It's beautiful to see Angie taking a cock in both ends at the same time, and so clearly enjoying every minute of it. Her vivacious red lipstick is smearing across her face and leaving a ring around Rick's shaft, and with every thrust from Jimmy, her mouth is pushed further on to the cock in her mouth, until she's taking all its length, her lips distended around its base and her nose brushing his wiry pubic hair.

Dan and I are openly jacking ourselves off as we watch what is happening in front of us, but Geoff has kept his cock firmly in his trousers. 'Come on, don't be shy. Show us what you've got,' I urge him, but as he unzips his trousers and drops them and his boxer shorts down to his knees, my words die in my throat. Quite simply, Geoff has the biggest cock I've ever seen – it must have been ten inches long, and as thick around as my forearm. The thought of *my* wife taking something that size inside her makes me feel sick with envy, but I can't stop rubbing my own erection as I stare at it. With a groan, Rick announces that he is coming. I imagine Rick holding her firmly by the hair, forcing to take every drop down her throat. This is the rough treatment my wife has craved, and she's patently loving it. Jimmy follows a couple of minutes later, his thrusting movements speeding up and his balls slapping against Angie's ass before he jerks and explodes inside her. Dan almost shoves Jimmy unceremoniously out of the way in his eagerness to take his turn. Jimmy simply moves Angie's head and presents his wilting cock to her mouth, ordering her to suck it clean. She's sucking at the mixture of his spunk and her cunt juice with obvious relish, as Dan slips his six rigid inches of cock flesh inside her. I carry on wanking as I watch Dan fuck Angie without any effort at all. His hands are gripping her hips and banging into her ferociously. By now, I'm close to coming in fantasy and reality, and I imagine going to stand in front of Angie, who is thrusting hard back on to Dan's cock, eyes closed in ecstasy. My come arcs out of my cockhead, the first jet landing in Angie's hair, the second and third splattering her cheek and already filthy lips, making her look like the come-hungry slut that I dream of.

Dan groans and comes, and I expect Jimmy to take his place, but Jimmy has other ideas. I'm already hard again, and he orders Angie to take his cock between her tits. She kneels up and removes her bra, pushing her breasts forward to envelop Jimmy's cock. As it slides back and forth in a mixture of his spittle and her cleavage sweat, I position myself underneath her so her freshly fucked pussy is above me. I have never tasted another man's spunk before, but I lick the salty mixture from her cunt without complaint. Jimmy lasts longer this time, but at last I hear him give out a groan as his spunk oozes out on to my wife's tits. 'While you're down there, mate,' I hear him say, as I continue to tongue Angie's pussy, 'lick her asshole, too. We're going to have her in every hole before we leave.' His words cause my cock, which has been slowly growing once more as I licked my wife out, to spring back to full hardness. And when Jimmy drags Geoff over by the arm, I realise just whose cock will be going up my wife's forbidden passage. 'He's never done a woman up the ass before,' Jimmy announces, 'but he's going to love it, aren't you, mate?' As he urges Geoff to lie on the floor, Angie gets a look at the lad's dick for the first time, and her eyes widen in fear and amazement. I, too, am unsure how she's going to get something that size into her tight anal hole, but Dan has spotted the pat of butter which Angie had placed on the table to accompany the crackers and cheese she had been serving. Geoff smothers his shaft with some of the butter, while Rick spreads the rest around and into my wife's anus. Egged on by his mates, he slips a finger inside her with a squelch, then a second. There was complete silence in the room; it seemed like we were all holding our breath as Rick slowly worked a third finger into Angie's ass. She seems to be in some discomfort at first, but as she grows used to the penetration she begins to relax, and soon he is able to push a fourth finger into her, and move his hand gently back and forth.

Geoff has overcome any nerves he has been feeling and is now eager to fuck my wife's ass. Almost reverentially, Dan and Jimmy help place Angie over Geoff's skyward-pointing erection and slowly lower her till she's impaled on his cock. Then they let go, and allow gravity to do its work until her anal passage is packed with solid flesh. She's still wearing the slutty split-crotch knickers and her stockings, which are ripped and laddered, and the streaks of dried come on them and her face add to her well-fucked, used appearance. I have never been so turned on as I am watching her slide herself up and down gingerly on Geoff's massive cock. The other lads are wanking themselves furiously until, one by one, they come, decorating her tits, shoulders and face with strings of spunk. Finally, Geoff announces that he, too, is coming, and Angie screams in pleasure as his cock shoots its load deep inside her. Again, I have the task of licking her to completion, come running out of her widely stretched asshole into my mouth. Come to think of it, I think Angie might be keen on a gang-bang after all!

* * *

- Here is one of the fantasies I received which was written in short-story form. I thought it was of sufficient quality to ask the writer if he felt he had a full-length erotic novel in him. He's excerpted again later in Chapter 4.

Damn it! All the bathroom cubicles had had their locks removed, against drug use, and Becky was dying for a wank on her way out of work.

Swallowing her reservations and, in truth, feeling a *frisson* of excitement at the possibility of discovery, Becky put her bag on the cubicle floor and threw her mac over the top of the door frame to hold the door closed. She stood and looked for a second. This would of course give away her identity away should anyone, unknown to her, overhear the shuffling and *sotto voce* groaning of her illicit wank. She removed it, propped the door closed and hoped for the best. As she bent to close the lid and sit on the pan, the residual stench of pee overpowered her. *You filthy slut, Becky*, she thought to herself, *you've no shame, shutting yourself in this feral-smelling little shithouse just to get off, you wanton little whore.* She slid off her flattie shoes and felt the cold hard floor on the soles of her feet, the hard lip of the toilet lid digging into the soft globes of her ass. Reaching into her bag, she brought out the stationery she had squirrelled away before lying back until she felt the hard edge of the cistern beneath her shoulder blades.

Undoing the upper buttons of her shirt, she pulled it away from her breasts and kneaded them through the silky fabric of her bra. She liked to see her nipples harden underneath some soft film, betraying her horniness beneath the propriety of their cover, and she flicked at them and began to pinch them cruelly before moving her arms wider to give herself tender little pinches all over her belly and sides. Then, returning to her tits, she peeled the bra cups down and pulled them out and over them.

Taking two large paperclips, she bent the open ends gently to see that they would give. Then, cupping the underside of her left breast, she slid one of them over the dark bumpy skin of her areola and along her nipple, releasing it gingerly until it hung free. Its bite made her wince and she felt the muscles throughout her body tense as she bore the pain for the moments it took to turn to pleasure. She was bearing it, and with that thought the sensation became a tingling numbness, a slow-burning but relentless one-way street – it was not allowed to come off until she had climaxed.

She gave her right breast treatment to match her left, and a couple of slaps for good measure, before slipping down the rasping zip at the side of her skirt and raising her hips to slide it down her legs and onto the floor, leaving her belt in place. With the shafts of tingling pain from her tits and the pulsing between her legs, she was growing impatient now, and she shoved the fat highlighter pen down the top of her tights but couldn't get anything like a satisfying angle. She teased her clit, drawing back its hood repeatedly with the side of the pen, its plastic quickly slick, but knew with frustration that she would have to stop again before she could continue.

She could carry on and, at length, come like this, but she craved it deeper, harder and quicker. Withdrawing the pen, she reached into her bag again and removed some nail scissors from her small collection of make-up. Tenting her tights in front of her knickers with the thumb and forefinger of her left hand, which still held the small bunch of elastic bands, she snipped at the mesh with the scissors in her right until a small hole appeared. Inserting her fingers, she ripped it wider with alacrity, the loud renting sound punctuating the silence of the toilets in testament to her depravity. Perhaps she should have gone to the trouble of removing them with her skirt, but the profligacy too was part of the thrill.

Easing her white cotton knickers to one side, she began to flick her distended clit fumblingly with an elastic band, sending out little shafts of pain that joined with those from her tormented nipples, before glancing down and stretching the rubber band vertically from the hood of her clit to her perineum until it banded her folds like the string on a joint of meat on a butcher's counter. Becky rubbed her sliver of flesh against the elastic band, holding the rubber still, making it dig painfully into the strengthening clit.

But her inventiveness had begun to flow further. She took the highlighter pen and three other elastic bands and wound them tightly around the plastic cylinder, leaving the others around her wrists, and creating three separate sets of firm ridges along the pen for her juicy quim to grip. Placing the device at the mouth of her pussy, she pushed about an inch of it gingerly up her, including the first ridge, enough for her to contract around and hold there while she gave her nipples further playful, painful twists, taking hold of the paperclips and rotating them sharply.

The pen looked so obscene sticking out of her, and her fanny looked so humiliatingly displayed, pulsing greedily around the pen, that she could hold back no longer, and she began to frig the pen in and out of her, gently at first and then with increasing punishment, and the tiled room filled with steady slicking sounds. Holding the cap firmly in her palm, she pushed the pen inside until her hand was flat against her quim, and arched her back still further, savouring her fullness.

Some of Becky's sexual imaginings had enough background to make a passable thriller, but in the impatience of the moment she cut to the chase – well, almost: she was perhaps a gangster's moll, and the two imposing, unforgiving lunks she pictured were his stooges, and she had wronged him, perhaps by an affair with a rival crook. Whatever, she was beneath contempt to him now, and he wouldn't even deign to punish her himself, handing her over to his yes-men instead, along with instructions – a perk of their job, like that film with Catherine Deneuve – *Belle de Jour*, that was it – except far, far seemier. They had bundled her roughly into this filthy toilet cubicle, away from prying eyes, where they would take their time with her.

Worked up now, Becky couldn't help but draw in the reek of stale urine with each sharp intake of breath and she was there, where she deserved to be, at the mercy of two calloused thugs who didn't know the meaning of the word, in a filthy cesspit toilet, fully dressed but not for long. One man was black and hulking, the other tall, blond and cold. The black guy whipped his belt out through his belt loops and, folding it in two in front of her with fury and resolve, struck her across the breasts just once as encouragement not to resist.

He spun her round, hair flying, and pushed her into the cubicle wall face-first, her cheek pressed against the cold tile, while the taller guy looked on, smiling. Expertly, the thicker man slid an arm through both of hers, pulling them up behind her so that she thrashed pathetically at his sides with her wrists and hands, able to move them only from the elbows down. Laughing now, he pushed his knee between her legs, pulling her skirt taut at each calf so that she could only twist and thrash her legs rather than kick him effectively.

He wrapped his belt around her wrists and pulled it tight enough to make her squeal. Still smiling, the white man passed his own belt to his companion, who knelt, more leisurely now she was clearly under their control, and threaded it in a figure of eight around her ankles. Then they threw her trussed form down like a sack so that she was sitting on the toilet facing them, silent now. Looking up, she noticed that the white man was leaning on the wall, his eyes shining, behind the black man who was advancing on her, grinning from ear to ear.

He took her by the collar of her shirt. She imagined the tearing, pinging sounds it would make as he ripped it down the front, almost pulling her off the pan with his force. The blond guy advanced too and put the palm of his hand to her chin, gripping her clenched jaw, raising her head sharply and forcing her to look him in the eyes. 'The boss tells me you're a filthy slut. What are you?'

'A filthy slut.'

'Again . . .'

'A filthy slut.' For a second, Becky thought she might really have said the words out loud. At least she flushed with an excited shame as if she had.

In the fantasy she was braless beneath her blouse, and the teutonic man ran his other hand down her neck. She felt his fingers, cold like a blade, snake down between her helpless orbs, which jiggled with her efforts to ease the sharp pains in her wrists from the tourniquet-tight belt which lashed them behind her back. The black guy's eyes fell hungrily upon them.

'It's not like us I know, but we're going to perform a little public service . . .'

'Wh . . . What do you mean?'

'Sort of a Surgeon General's warning . . .' With that, he knelt in front of her, placing a knee to prevent her kicking out her bound legs as one, and cupped the underside of her left breast, giving her nipple a cursory twist, while his broader companion covered her mouth with a giant hand, placing the other on the back of her head and pushing it sharply down until she was forced to watch her own tits. 'By the way, you're trussed up for your own good, because if you thrash around then we're just going to have to punish you for that, too.' With the binding on her arms pulling them out behind her, her tits were pronounced, their fine tawny flesh stretched taut.

The cubicle filled with the musk of Becky's excitement. In her fantasy it was fear. The white guy produced a tube of lipstick – where did that come from? Becky hurriedly included her bag in the fantasy – and twisted the base until the waxy red column rose a little, not enough to break off when he pushed it hard into the upper slope of her right breast. With the concentration of a jeweller, the blond man drew it along her right breast, pausing to twist more out. In angular letters, straight but messy lines, he scrawled an 'S' and an 'L', before turning to her left breast for the 'U' and the 'T'. The black guy's middle finger had snaked into her gasping mouth and she sucked on it in her shame.

Then the black guy slid his hands under her armpits and lifted her, pulling her arms slightly further back, making her cleavage gape. They spun her, whimpering, to face the toilet and pushed her over the bowl, her knees on the pee-soaked floor and her monikered tits squashed against the closed lid.

The broad black guy had slipped off his suit jacket and now, with a ping, took off the braces he was wearing. He pulled them around the back of her flailing head and crossed them, knotting them loosely at her throat before fastening the crossed ends around the outflow pipe where it joined the toilet pan, so that she would not choke but her head was forced down, practically kissing the outside of the porcelain through the cascading hair that covered her upside-down face. (Frigging herself fetidly with the high-lighter pen and twisting the paperclips on her poor sore nipples, Becky had decided that the toilet in her fantasy would be as acrid as the one on which she really sat, with only herself as her torturer.)

Now the two thugs appraised her. 'Shit,' the white guy said, 'toilets're always blocked around here.' Unable to raise herself at all, her ass prone to their view beneath her bound arms jutting above it, she heard him pull down his zip and felt the sole of his large foot press down on her back. His urine spattered with force on the nape of her neck, cascading through her hair and falling in droplets on the floor beneath her. Her flesh almost stung with humiliation. A little of the stream trickled its way to her poor tits, squashed on the toilet lid.

As the torrent lessened, she sensed the broader man behind her, impatient now, done with games. As his companion removed his foot, he took hold of the hem of her skirt and wrenched it up until it bunched at her waist, then wrenched her knickers away from her stockinged legs until they dug painfully into her abdomen before ripping apart. She heard him spit copiously into his hand and felt him rub the saliva around her anal whorl. Crudely, the black guy inserted an exploratory finger into her moistened pucker. 'I'm going first . . .'

Becky plunged the highlighter pen into herself more recklessly than ever as she imagined how her two hoods would bugger her without mercy, thrashing and grunting as they took turns, bickering for her hole like it was a commodity that existed for their pleasure alone, treating her as nothing more than a receptacle, no more than the reeking toilet to which she had seen herself held fast.

As she imagined herself straining against her bonds in abject fear, her orgasm began, spasming outward and sending shivers through her, until there was nothing in her mind but the shame she pictured scrawled onto her tits and the stench of urine in her nostrils, not the sound of the pen slicking in and out of her quim, nor her sharp panting, nor the telltale rustle of her clothing. She conjured her sense of restriction and panic still harder, imagining her bonds digging into her flesh as she held the pen still and rode her peak, gripping it harder than ever, twisting and slapping a paperclipped nipple into the bargain. Deliciously, the tension flooded out of her and she kept her eyes closed for a few moments, laying her head back on the cistern as she came to rest.

The pain of the clips on her nipples was getting too much, out of context all of a sudden, but she'd bear it for a few moments more, she thought. She brought her head forward and, opening her eyes lazily, took in the skirt at her feet and her wantonly ripped tights, wishing now that she'd really had the stockings she'd given herself in her fantasy. The modified pen sat in her hand, and both were slicked with a white viscous sheen. She was almost surprised to see that her breasts, save her nipples, were unharmed, their unblemished skin framed by her pulled-down bra.

But as she raised both hands to unhook the paperclips from her poor punished areolae, teats engorged with blood choked off by the metal, her life seemed to stand still. She saw the bottom of the door in the corner of her vision, where it shouldn't be – it was open! In a flash she looked up to see Maddy, her dykey New Yorker boss, standing before her, her hands on her ample hips, her expression at once candid and quizzical, with a smile which became a leer as she caught Becky's eye.

Becky could not hold her gaze in the moment of silence that followed, during which her heart crashed through the floor and her cheeks ran hot as if Maddy had not only caught her wanking but had read her shameful thoughts as well. She pictured herself as Maddy must see her – her improvised tit clamps betraying her filthy, fiendish mind and her ripped hose her wantonness. For the first time she noticed how sweaty she had become, too. No doubt in vain, she closed her hand around the highlighter pen.

And all the time Maddy's face was fixed with that 'I've got you' grin. When she spoke, her tone betrayed nothing about what exactly she was going to do about it. 'You're an inventive little minx, Becky Bunbury. Let's have a word in my office when you've ... erm ... composed yourself.' And with that, she turned away.

Becky felt as if she really did have 'slut' scrawled onto her tits.

Becky stayed in the cubicle a while longer, her fearful encounter with Maddy having encouraged her to use it for its intended purpose. Her mind was a welter of mixed feelings – on the one hand, her job at the magazine would never be quite the same, if she was allowed to keep it. And even if she was, she should chance it and move on anyway. And perhaps her evening with Jim would be a hurried mess now. What if Maddy made her stay?

On the other hand, she felt like a naughty school-girl at one of those exclusive private places, waiting outside the headmistress's study, and it excited her. If she weren't such a slave to her paranoia she might have admitted that Maddy's expression betrayed excitement too. Hell, the old frowse was probably diddling herself behind her desk right now.

Becky crossed the office to curious looks from a couple of gossipy staffers and, her heart beating hard in her chest, rapped on Maddy's door. 'Come in,' said Maddy, like the spider to the fly. As Becky stood before her, she felt her shame colour her cheeks. Maddy leaned back in the leather office chair, a heel on her desk. She didn't invite Becky to sit. 'That lie was the only white thing about you, wasn't it.'

Becky was taken aback. 'Wh ... what lie?' So she was going to take full advantage, the bitch.

105

'About the show tonight, about you going home to rest up for that. Something tells me you're not going to see any band tonight. Am I right?'

Becky should have been affronted, should have slammed her fist on the desk and told her where to stuff her job, and that she'd see her in court. This was litigious California, after all. But the thought of waving the complimentary tickets – that she had no intention of using – in Maddy's face seemed in bad faith, and something in Maddy's voice compelled her to go along with the way the older woman was playing this. 'Yes,' she said, almost under her breath.

'And what are you doing instead?'

'Don't really know. This guy I've been seeing –'

'Don't know? That could mean a candlelit supper, but from the little I know about you, Becky Bunbury, I'd say that wasn't really your style. Is it some kind of scene? If not, I bet you wish it was. You're a little bit submissive, right?'

Becky gulped, 'G . . . guess so, I –'

Maddy threw her head back in triumph. 'Thought so from the stationery I saw on your nipples.' Becky gasped. Uncomfortably aware of the feral scent left from her frenzied masturbation – she hadn't exactly had her mind on tidying up – and shocked at how fast this was moving, she coloured further. 'Hardly much point in having your shirt buttoned up now, is there? Does he parade around you in leather pants, this man, brandishing a whip?'

'Not yet.' Through her humiliation, Becky had to admit she felt a wave of relief that whatever this was, at least it wasn't official business after all.

'Forgive my intrusiveness, Rebecca, I just want to get a . . . erm . . . full picture of you. And, contrary to the gossip round here I don't mind men, especially ones who let me in on their femme little girlfriends. Is this . . .'

'Jim.'

'Jim, right. Is he like that?' And from behind her desk she raised one of her shoes, more of a slipper really. 'No matter – if not, what he doesn't know won't hurt him . . .' Holding it by the heel so that its sole flexed in a whiplike arc, she brought the shoe down with a crack on her desk '. . . will it.' Becky caught her eyes and saw the smile within them, in contrast to the stern set of her face. Becky went with it. Maddy knew she could storm out of there, but instead she let her eyes drop to the floor, giving Maddy licence to continue.

Emboldened, Maddy unplugged the phone, twisted the sun blind closed until the room was darker, private, intimate, and walked imperiously around to stand behind Becky. 'You never give away anything you don't really want to give away, you know. Seeing you in that bathroom only confirmed for me what a filthy little whore you are. You've set me a problem, you see. I can't keep my mind on my work now. I've got to get you out of my system, and filthy, self-centred submissives like you just revel in their own humiliation, whoever it comes from. There's only one stance I can take on this . . .' With that, she spread her legs wider and flexed her knees, swivelling at the hips like a golfer taking a swing. 'Effective action.' Becky gasped as the shoe sliced the air behind her.

'Now, I'm going to time my strokes, ten seconds between them, so you can ruminate on your shame while you await the next one, while my eyes drink you in. If I had a cane or a crop then you'd get away with six, but with this lousy flat sole I better make it twenty, to give a little hussy like you the lesson she really deserves. Oh, and that skirt is far too thick. It'll have to come up.' And with that, she grabbed the hem and bunched it crudely around Becky's waist just as she had imagined the burly thug doing, back in the toilet that had brought her to this. Becky gasped.

'I see you've got elastic bands around your wrists . . . how practical for a little wannabe sex-slave like you.' Becky was dumbfounded – she had forgotten about them, and Maddy's deadpan delivery only intensified her shame, causing excitement to flicker anew. 'Now take them and twist them into a figure of eight. Make sure both wrists are stuck through them. They're less than you deserve, but I don't want a hand flying round to shield your sweet curves from their just desserts, do I.'

Becky fumbled, figuring out the best way to accomplish it, not fast enough for Maddy, who brought her shoe down hard on the base of her buttocks. 'Do it! And that was extra.' The surprise caused Becky's body to straighten to its fullest, taller than Maddy now, but then a colt was also bigger than its trainer, and that didn't help it much. 'Now bend over and put those bound wrists on the edge of my desk, and if you straighten up at all, it's another ten strokes . . . One.' And with that, she brought the shoe down hard on her ass again, the skin of Becky's globes tautened under her ripped tights now that she was bending. Becky felt the elastic of her knickers, framing her buttocks like a target, containing them as a sharp pain shot through them, making her wince and squeal.

Becky tried to count to ten and time the next blow, feeling Maddy's hungry eyes on her. The older woman was no doubt appreciating how pronounced her ass now was, and how her breasts had jiggled at the stroke. She was exhibited now, like a slave in a market, goods in a shop window. She felt watched as if through glass, and a shiver of arousal ran through her.

She would not straighten, would not! As the measured blows continued until the stinging had spread and diffused into a general soreness, like an intensified flush of shame, Becky found it harder each time not to bring herself up straight, and she rubbed her sheathed legs together, rustling her tights and jiggling her buttocks to displace the urge. Her own participation really turned her on – by setting her the task of staying prone, Maddy had made her complicit in her sluttish degradation.

She was smelling ever ranker, and her quim lips were rubbing together with her spent juices from before. In the silence between the seventh and eighth stroke, Becky heard Maddy groan softly, and the telltale sound of a finger rubbing a moist clit. She had pulled open the buttons of her combat pants. The sense of Maddy standing there, just staring, appraising her nubility as if she were a fine vase, made Becky ache to frig her own clit once more. So aware of being watched, and deliciously fearful of the consequences of moving, Becky gingerly inched her own bound wrists back from the desk towards the rent in her tights.

Before she reached it, however, Maddy almost bellowed, 'Damn, woman. Can't you do anything you're told?' Becky's fingers clawed the air, frozen on their trajectory towards her moistening cunt. 'Alright, you can frig yourself like the lowly whore you are but remember, this problem-solving session is about solving *mine*, and your own tawdry pleasure takes a back seat. Remember that.' Beneath the apparent severity of her words, Becky could tell from her tone that Maddy was gratified that she was turning her on.

Becky's own clit was aflame, her mind free of images this time – her real-life shame more than enough – and she wasted no time in making use of the permission she'd been given to bring herself off. But the measuredness of the strokes was almost infuriating – both women were frigging themselves with unselfconscious abandon now, but still Maddy made sure that her shoe cut the air to land on Becky's ass only between even counts of ten. Concentrating the blow always in the same place, sparing her no variation and ensuring that the area just above the crease at the top of her legs was burning raw, Maddy seemed to be making time itself stretch out, gazing at Becky ever more intently between strokes. It was a steady, inexorable, gruelling journey that Becky wouldn't have stopped for anything right then.

But stop it did – at the seventeenth stroke, Maddy cried out behind her, a curiously delicate whimper, as if she didn't want Becky to be a part of her orgasm, then let out a long sigh. She waited a few moments and then she delivered the eighteenth spank, almost cursorily, and Becky felt almost jilted as the tension in the room diminished palpably.

Then she understood – Maddy didn't want her to come after all. She had worked her up to a point of no return and now came Becky's real punishment – to face what a wanton little slut she was, with no relief from Maddy, used and cast aside to make her way home frustrated, as thrown back once more on her own devices as she had been in the toilet in which she'd so obscenely been caught. And Maddy had got off on the thought.

Seeing Maddy's fiendishness so starkly sent a thrill through her anew. As she gloried in the game of attrition, Becky knew she had to come. She must! As the nineteenth and penultimate stroke sliced the air to land on her reddened cheeks, she knew what she had to do: Becky would just about have time to get off if she gratified Maddy with the true depths of her wantonness, giving her consent to a final round of humiliation. So taken aback at first, now she could not let her pride get in the way of an orgasm at the hands of this imperious woman, an amazon with even so humble an instrument of torture as an office shoe. Seizing the moment, she stood up petulantly to her fullest height.

'Ha! I knew it!' Maddy cooed triumphantly. 'If you want your ass peppered that hard, little girl, then you're more of a glutton than even I took you for. Is there no end to your cravenness?' And with that, Maddy forgot her measuredness. She advanced on Becky and rained blows on her poor sore ass until there was no point in either of them keeping count.

Lost in a welter of surprise and sensation, Becky felt the target area widen to include the sides of her ass and her thighs. She heard the shoe clunk to the floor and felt Maddy's hand continue the work – forehand and backhand, like she were playing squash, with the occasional squeeze and pinch that sent shafts of tender pain through to Becky's clit. Her fingers scrabbled at her pussy with abandon, driven by the desperate and exhilarating fear that Maddy still might just stop at any moment and throw her back on her own humiliation. 'Oh God, please don't stop. Don't stop . . . Don't stop . . .' She begged over and over, the phrase like a mantra, confession and propitiation of her shame.

Becky rode the blows to her own shuddering orgasm, stronger for being her second in only a little while. As she came, Maddy leaned towards her ear and breathed in a stage whisper, husky and low, 'You filthy . . . little . . . fucking . . . whore. You . . . filthy . . . little . . . fucking . . . slut,' raining blows until Becky's climax subsided and her ass burned in agony all of a sudden. Her words had joined with Becky's in a brief opera of domination that had pushed the younger woman over the brink.

Tears of relief and pain welled in Becky's eyes and she collapsed across her boss's desk, her face turned away. Maddy curled her body around her new-found plaything's prostrate form and reached out a tender hand to brush her dark hair away from her cheek. 'Come over to the couch,' she said, her voice soft and reassuring, and Becky let her lead her there. Maddy cuddled her, folding her arms around her, clearing the hair from around Becky's freckled face and raising it to hers with a finger under the chin, tender now and concerned at Becky's flushed, tear-stained face. 'So . . . you wanna get a coffee?'

4

Domination

Hapless moppets, CP and humiliation

- Nexus believes in safe, sane and consensual sex.
- Remember – these are fantasies. For a responsible guide to the practice of SM/CP, which touches on the emotional issues involved, try *SM101* by Jay Wiseman, Greenery Press (2nd edn. 1996).

A favourite fantasy: I am living somewhere warm in a moderately big house, I keep three or four young or very young (teenage) women there much as I now keep dogs, I give them food and exercise (esp. tennis), educate them somewhat, but provide no clothes, they are always naked, it's pleasant for me but so usual it's like having pretty wallpaper; I too am most of the time naked. Since (in this dream) it is miserable to go to sleep or to wake up without an erection, I sleep between two of them, fondling Miss Left at night while Miss Right plays with my prick and balls. Miss Right in the morning . . .; I remember my manners and while I am always making comparisons mentally, do not speak them aloud. Each afternoon, outdoors, I have full intercourse with a third, the fourth that day attends to cooking and other domestic tasks – by some kind of rota I have much variety.

* * *

I am responding to the advert you placed in issue forty of *Desire Direct*, which said, 'Mass Market UK publisher wants to hear your sexual fantasies and offers a sex novel as an inducement. 'Stocks permitting' I understand is a get-out clause which lets you renege on that idea. Despite the possibility of being disappointed by you, here is what I offer you.

Her husband took her to sit at the picnic table even though there was an older man sat there cleaning his Nikon camera and lenses. They sat facing this man. She knew the stranger had some standing in the field of photography for only the most dedicated bought and used Nikon cameras.

Obediently she removed her jacket, blushing a bright scarlet, for she saw the stranger was aware she wore no bra and her nipples were pierced for rings to be worn there. The dark material of her top made that fact certain, for it enhanced her breasts rather than hid them, being as it was almost transparent and dark.

She unpacked the food and alcohol even as her partner broke the silence by asking serious questions about the stranger's interest in photography. All three realised, fairly quickly, her husband wanted to know the level of the photographer's abilities *and* when it was seen to border on a professional standing the talk turned to the thoughts of the stranger, concerning the legalities of sexual posing.

The photographer pointed out that public displays of nudity were a matter for the photographer and the 'model' *but* all efforts should be made to ensure the 'nudity' did not embarrass innocent people who might pass. That answer led her husband to say, 'Claire here is a submissive female, ready to pose in any of the poses I want, *but* we cannot find a photographer to take the photos I want. What would you want to take the photos I want of her?'

Claire looked up at the stranger when he said, directly, to her, 'If I may be so bold, Claire, do you really want to pose for photos requested by your partner?' The baritone voice carried tones of sincere regard for her feelings as well as suppressed excitement. The strength of that voice and concern let Claire look him straight in the eye and say, 'My husband is also my master. My greatest pleasure is to please him as and how I can. Posing for a camera seems of little consequence.'

She trembled at the stranger's response for he made it clear that *he* thought her husband was going to ask for some *very* adult poses from her *and* those poses *might* include her facing pain, humiliation and bouts of sexual frustration.

With head held high, Claire said, 'What my husband and master *asks* of me is seen as a command I must obey. If you wish to be the photographer do not fret over my wellbeing but say you agree to use your photographic knowledge to create the best possible poses asked of me.' Her reply let the stranger turn to her husband/master and say what his 'price' would be.

It pleased Claire to find the price was nothing more than fullest sexual use of Claire's mouth, fanny and arse, during and after the shoot was done *and* he agreed to begin the shoot immediately he had some lunch. What had been a picnic for two now became a three-person lunch.

While they ate the food and demolished the wine, the photographer listened to her husband's ideas *and* felt able to set Claire into her first pose, there at the table.

Claire was asked to sit on the table's top while her master sat between her spread thighs and rested his forearms on her thighs. All could see that the pose denied Claire the chance to close her legs, yet anyone passing would see little of her secret places because her master's body blocked that aspect of the view she gave him. The scene they portrayed was of a couple intent upon each other and unaware of other people. Only her husband could see, for sure, that Claire wore no panties and had shaved her crotch (to a hair-free zone), just a couple of hours ago.

When there were no others to note the two men swapped places and the photographer caught a very sharp close-up of Claire's bared and shaven haven seen clearly under her mid-thigh-length skirt. Though he liked what he captured on film, the stranger set her man back in that first position, stepped back from them and set himself to capture a shot which showed Claire's nipple-ringed breasts *and* her shaven haven in the same shot. He used the side of her husband's head and his shoulder line to frame the shot, seen from behind her man, but seeing all that he could see of Claire's special 'picnic preparation' work and pose.

They moved on to other poses, such as Claire, alone, set in the centre of the tabletop. Claire was asked to dangle one knee off the table while the other knee was raised. To his order she rested her chin on the upturned knee and thought over some fantasy of her own. It was made clear that her 'daydreamer' look would make it look as if she was innocently unaware that she was showing her love crease to anyone who dared to look more closely.

Claire lay flat on her back, allowing the photographer to stand over her and shoot down while she thought sexy thoughts and looked straight up at him. The idea was made easier for Claire when she saw the prominent bulge at his thigh and imagined being sexual with him. That thought made her re-examine the stranger. He was older than the two of them and no Robert Redford look-alike *but* that cock was worth a second look.

She felt her love lips weep with suppressed lust even as she guessed it to be around the eight inches mark, with a two-inch diameter. She wondered how it would stretch her mouth *and* feel pulsing, in the back of her throat, while she coped with the ejaculation of the love fluids she must swallow.

With all three in a state of high arousal the shot was easily captured *but* her increased arousal brought the same increase to that of her two males *and* so the poses became more blatant and the risk of passers by were an ignored feature.

This was the moment her husband sprang his first surprise on Claire. From his trousers he drew a pair of rubber pants, which he handed her and asked her to get into. As she unfolded them all saw the two built-in sex toys attached to the pants *and* knew, Claire was being asked to fit those toys into her love cave and anal passage *while* the men watched her do so.

The camera man delayed the fitting by asking her to climb on to the table and slowly go through the fitting so that he could capture her fitting the pants over one ankle; shoot the sight of those two toys nudging her calves and as they vanished into their respective holes. Claire saw the males give their own signs of approval when she stretched the rubber pants tightly over her lower belly and spread her legs wide.

She stood near the edge of the table so the camera man could lay on his back, looking up between her thighs and focus his camera on her rubbery gusset, capturing clear evidence that she was toy-filled front and rear.

Her husband made it clear that he was in need of sexual relief and the camera man said he was not alone in that hunger for sexual relief. Their responses made Claire feel proud and there was a three-way agreement to the suggestion that they tidy away their picnic remains and get home for some sex fun.

As Claire walked in the middle of the threesome, she regularly reached down to check her men still hungered for her. She was unashamedly thinking of what awaited her when they got home.

She was keen on the idea of taking one man orally while a second thrust into her, from the rear. Her love juices flowed ever more copiously as she gave the image free rein and that free thinking led her to imagine herself finding that oral cock pushed ever deeper down her throat. Though she knew such actions would cause her to choke on that invading 'lollipop' she yearned for the scene to be lived out.

At the town square clock, she saw the time and that made her think of how much time there was for fun to be had. There were quite a few hours to live out before bedtime and she saw those hours as the source of many sexual pleasures. By the time she reached the front door the wildest scene she could imagine was to have one male laid on the carpet so she could straddle his hips, fill her love crease with his cock and lean forward so the second cock could fill and fuck her back passage.

Such thoughts made her hands shake and the unlocking of the door took longer than she wanted *but* she knew each of the three was hungering for the real thing. Even as she unlocked the front door the silliest thought she wondered was how she could ever, from this day forward, think of picnics as simply an out of doors lunch-break without blushing a deep scarlet at this memory.

I chose to stop here *because* this seems like a natural ending to the picnic scene and the beginning of indoor fun options *she* may not have considered.

Not being an author I do not believe I can give this the depth or length that would turn it from a short fantasy into a decently long 'Chapter 1'. I do see how Claire has not been given any 'body' to make her sexy, sad or whatever *and* her husband is even less fleshed out. However, if you see this fantasy as having some 'book value' share the idea with an author who can strengthen Chapter 1 and take it on from here.

I think I have made it clear that Claire is going to be bondage-held so that she can be both rewarded and punished for the sake of the photographs that can be had from such activities. I do have some very dramatic scenes as well as a striking bedtime scene in mind *but* there are hours to write about before that 'scene' is required.

If you are interested in knowing more of my ideas feel free to ask me to write them out for you. The ideas are 'video used as a warning to behave'. She can be posed in bondage while standing, sitting, kneeling, laid flat and hog-tied. Each pose lets the binder show how she can be teased sexually *and* punished. My wildest ever ideas are to turn a female into a 'Human Reading Lamp' or a 'Human Drinks Trolley' and the annoying thing is, with work, I believe they could become real creations to be used by some dominant partners.

* * *

I imagine my girlfriend and I have just been to our first private SM party, fulfilling a long-standing fantasy of mine. We have been going to fetish clubs for a couple of years now, and in my fantasy we're invited to a couples-only party at a big country house just outside of London. I have always been the dominant one in our relationship, and Stella is my submissive slave, which suits us both.

We arrive feeling nervous and excited about what's going to happen. We've both dressed for the occasion. I'm in tight leather trousers and heavy boots with lots of buckles, and a black fishnet top that shows off the ring in my left nipple. Stella's in six-inch stilettos and fishnet stockings attached to a PVC suspender belt, together with a PVC bra that leaves her pierced nipples uncovered. I have not allowed her the luxury of panties. Her pussy has been shaved for the occasion, and a small brass padlock has been attached to the piercings in her labia. I'm led into one room where I can socialise and drink with the other doms, while she's taken to another room, where the slaves, both male and female, are left to get to know each other. Like I say, I've been to fetish clubs, but this would be something different. The couples would be broken up straight away, letting them know this was completely out of the ordinary.

Then each slave would be taken into the room where all action was about to occur. The idea is that they would all be put through their paces in turn, so that the doms can see how well trained and obedient they are. I know how humiliating it would be for Stella to have me punish her in front of everyone else, and that's why the idea appeals so. And there's always the chance that some other master or mistress would want to punish her, too, and I'd have no objection. Stella would be terrified at the coming ordeal, and yet at the same time know she couldn't lose face. Of necessity almost, she'd feel herself starting to get wet, her sex lips pushing against the restraints of the little padlock, the symbol of her being my possession and obsession, in anticipation of the pain and pleasure to come.

Finally, Stella is taken into the main room. There'd be a dozen or so people in there, and she's glancing round nervously at the expectant audience, wondering who they are and thinking how much they're relishing her shame. As she passes the leather- and rubber-clad doms, she can hear crude comments about the size of her breasts, and her shaven pussy, and bets being made as to how much punishment she'll be able to take. They discuss her like she's not there.

Her hands, which were cuffed together while she waited, are released, and I step forward to bend her slight body over a padded whipping stool in the middle of the room. Then I fasten her wrists securely to the far side of the stool, undo the padlock with a snick, and spread her legs crudely, holding them in place with a spreader bar at the ankles, to make sure she cannot rise or flinch too far from me. I think of her knowing she is so completely open and vulnerable, and that anyone behind me has a good view of her moist pink sex and puckered rosebud. The audience are crowding round more closely, ready to see how well she has been trained, and the thought of being looked at so intimately only serves to make her even more conspicuously wet. I walk in front of her, so she can see that I'm holding a riding crop – her least favourite instrument of discipline because it's the one that hurts the most, and at this she knows that I really mean to test her. Her breasts are hanging forward in front of the stool, defenceless, and I use the end of the crop to tease her nipples, bringing them to full hardness. She moans softly.

Then the punishment begins. I move behind her, and tap her bottom gently with the crop, measuring the distance of my swing, and so as not to catch Stella too unawares. The crop whistles through the air, then lands square across her bum cheeks. If I'm feeling merciful, I'll warm her up first, bringing my strokes – whether with palm or instrument – gradually up to strength, but in my fantasy I lay them right on. She yelps and bucks in her bonds, but is restrained so securely that she can barely move. What intimacies for a roomful of strangers to be witnessing! I give her a moment to recover from the shock of that blow, and then follow up with a second, parallel to the first. Another line of fire must have sprung up on her tenderised flesh, for she's mewing now, incoherently. But I'm oblivious to her pleas, she knows the safe-word. As I never let her take fewer than six strokes in a session, she knows how many she has left to endure. Again and again the crop falls, welting her skin. I'm careful to place the strokes so that each one covers a new area, gradually moving lower until I catch the fleshy underhang of her bum, dangerously close to her vulnerable pussy lips. She shrieks as the stroke hits home, but the agony is now answered with a tingle of pleasure, and despite being stuck fast in position, she's beginning to feel the need to come.

Satisfied that I have punished her enough, I now decide it's time to reward Stella, but only on condition that she begs for her pleasure like the slut she is. In front of everyone there, she has to tell me that she needs to have her cunt and bum fingered. I tell her only sluts take pleasure in what had just been done to her, but that she was my slut, and if she would do anything I wanted, with anyone I wanted, then I'd always be there to make her come. I drop the crop, and begin to run my hands over her well-striped bottom. My finger moves lower, down into her juicy crease. I circle her clitoris with my thumb for a moment, causing her to groan with pleasure, then insert first one, then two fingers into her cunt, thrusting them slowly in and out. Restrained as she is, Stella can do very little to direct her own pleasure, but I know exactly what to do to make her come. But I'm stringing it out for the benefit of the watching crowd, not giving a toss about her pleasure, gradually stretching her further by adding more fingers. Eventually, she has three fingers in her cunt and my thumb in her bum hole, and she's crying out as my pistoning hand makes my index finger slide back and forth over the nubbin of her clit. As one of the watching doms reaches out a hand and tugs cruelly on one of her nipple rings, reminding her that the two of us are far from alone, that's it. She howls her pleasure, her body spasming and her muscles clenching around my now-slick fingers. The sheer humiliation of being made to come in front of so many people sinks in as Stella spends the rest of her evening back in her chains, her sore bum pressed uncomfortably against the cold wall and her labia padlocked together once more, while I repair to watch the rest of the entertainment.

I'm pleased to say this fantasy hasn't been too far from the reality sometimes. And there'd be no fun in punishing someone for me if she didn't get off on it. How else would you show her what a little slut she is?

* * *

I began to have this fantasy after my girlfriend was late a lot. I try to please her most of the time, and I don't really pull her up on things that get on my nerves about her. Among my friends, I've always been the late one, and had a reputation for it, so much so that it turned into a bit of a joke. When we first met, I inwardly rejoiced that I'd met someone who also knew what it was like to be the butt of that joke. Little did I know how crap she was at keeping time! It got to the point where I couldn't help but take it personally, like she didn't care enough about me.

I'm the one on the receiving end of this one flaw in the character of someone who is pretty, intelligent, kind and has the sort of body which makes other women jealous. Eventually, I suppose I was not prepared to tolerate it, but couldn't say so. Now I've always liked the fact that I've tended to wank while thinking about the girl I'm going out with, rather than some stranger. And these days I seem to be having variations of the following fantasy!

We arrange that Anna will arrive at my house by seven o'clock at the latest, so that we can be at the restaurant by eight. She has promised me faithfully she'll be on time, but as seven comes and goes, without any sign of her, I realise I have been stupid to believe that promise. When she finally does ring the doorbell, I'm sitting with a glass of whisky, pondering how best to teach her the lesson she so badly needs. I go to open the door and she breezes in without a word of apology.

'You realise I've had to ring and cancel the table, don't you?' I say.

'But I was looking forward to dinner,' Anna responds. 'I haven't eaten since breakfast and I'm starving.'

'Well, how was I to know what time you would turn up?' I retort. 'If you knew you were going to be running late, you could at least have called to let me know.'

'I'm sorry, Oliver, it won't happen again,' she says, lowering her head.

'I wish I could believe that,' I reply. 'There's only one way to make sure it doesn't, and I should have done this a long time ago. I'm afraid I'm going to have to spank some manners into you. I want you over my knee, now.'

'What?' Anna exclaims. 'You're kidding, aren't you?'

I shake my head. 'I've never been more serious.' I drag her, spluttering and coughing in indignation, to the armchair where I had been sitting nursing my drink while I waited for her to arrive. Anna is Welsh, only a little over five feet tall and barely weighs anything, so it's easy to haul her on to my lap. She struggles and tries to break free of my grip. But I'm resolutely serious in my intent, and that lends me the strength to hold her in place.

She is wearing a short black dress with a flared skirt, tulip-shaped. And when I flip the hem of that skirt out of the way to give me access to her backside, I almost laugh at my luck and her misfortune. The underwear she'd chosen – a skimpy white lace G-string and black hold-up stockings – had obviously been intended to turn me on when we got back from dinner. I have to confess they're doing their job now, my cock beginning to rise from its dormant state as I take in the delicious sight of her full, creamy ass cheeks, with the little strip of lace disappearing between them to divide her sex, but I know those skimpy panties would offer her no protection when I began to spank her. For all the area they cover, she might as well have been naked from the waist down.

'Forty minutes, wasn't it?' I say casually.

'What do you mean?' she asks.

'You were forty minutes late, I believe. I think forty spanks will help to bring the point home to you.'

I let her wait for a long moment, giving her time to mull over the implications of what I've just told her, before bringing my open palm down sharply on her youthful, pneumatic buttock, which wobbles a little with the impact. She gives a little anguished cry, as if surprised by the force of the blow, though in truth I have not actually hit her that hard, and I think her reaction is more one of indignation that in this day and age she is being treated this way.

After that little loosener, I really begin to spank her in earnest, my palm landing rapidly and methodically over every inch of exposed flesh. I watch the white handprint form on her skin, before the blood flows in to turn it red. Soon what had been pale flesh is a vibrant crimson, and Anna is wriggling and squirming on my lap, trying to get away from the relentless onslaught. Her frantic movements stimulate my cock, causing it to stiffen uncomfortably in the confines of my trousers.

As I carry on slapping her bottom, she begins to cry, softly at first, but soon fat teardrops are rolling down her cheeks to land on the carpet. Her carefully applied mascara is running, and tendrils of her long, black hair are sticking to her wet cheeks. She looks wretched and humiliated, and I find that even more of a turn-on.

I run an experimental finger over the taut gusset of her G-string, registering the damp feel of the fabric. When I slip that finger under the lace to touch the lips and folds of her pouting cunt, she moans and thrusts her pelvis back at me with an eagerness that takes me by surprise, wanting me to touch her more forcefully.

I pull my hand away, smiling at her groan of frustration, and give her the last five spanks. These are the hardest of all, and I have her squealing in pain as my hand lands with real spite on her tormented bum cheeks. Then, without ceremony, I push her off my lap and watch as she lands in a snivelling, dishevelled heap on the floor.

'Strip,' I tell her. 'I want you naked by the time I've got my cock out, or I may just have to add a couple more to what I've just given you.'

She scrabbles to pull off her dress, with none of the coquetry she had shown when I first announced her punishment. Anna has small, perfect breasts and seldom wears a bra, and so all she has to remove is her sodden G-string. I take a moment to savour the sight of her beautiful body, clad only in the hold-up stockings, then I present my now fully erect penis to her mouth and order her to suck. I'm excited, I almost come the moment her full, wet lips close around my swollen glans.

If I were still going in real life after all that, then in my imagination I'd order her to lie on her back and part her legs widely. I'd put the head of my cock at the entrance to her vagina and thrust home, feeling her tight, ribbed walls clinging possessively to my shaft, as if afraid I would withdraw it from them. I'd pound into her hard and fast, making her body slide back and forth on the carpet, knowing how this would be causing the rough fibres to scrape against her sore bum cheeks. I'd prod around her back and ass with my fingers, making sure I could feel the heat rising from her anguished skin. When I'd come, and she'd come, I'd ask her whether the spanking, and her flesh burning on the rug as we'd fucked afterwards, had turned her on. I'm almost to the point of thinking I should try this, past caring if it doesn't work. If she liked it, of course, it wouldn't change a thing about her being late, but at least it would give me an excuse to spank her!

* * *

I am a successful businessman in my early sixties, and used, I suppose, to getting exactly what I want. Since I met her last year, I've had a lighthearted thing about my finance director's wife. But I'd do nothing to spoil my relationship with him, or hurt him. I've also lived long enough to know that the reality seldom lives up to what the imagination makes of something, so I'd never do anything about it. I'd also want a really submissive woman now, because I'm finally old enough to know what I'm into, if I ever find it, and not mess about. And I don't know strictly whether she is, although she's really flirty. Nevertheless, I like to imagine that she's abjectly submissive. They've invited me out to dinner and although it's his call, I end up naming the venue. Assuring him it's within budget, I don't let on, however, that it's a very exclusive establishment – one in which he might end up parting with his wife, for a while, more than cash! Although something tells me he wouldn't mind anyway – we've grown close over the years, and they seem to have that kind of a relationship. He knows that tonight I want Gemma, and he is not going to stand in the way of my getting her. I know tonight will be a good opportunity to put Gemma through her paces, and to watch Jim's reaction as I do whatever I want to her.

Gemma would be told to dress for the occasion in a long scarlet coat-dress that buttoned all the way down the front. That would look stunning against her olive skin and dark, waist-length hair, and all she would wear beneath it would be sheer black stockings and suspenders. Black patent leather shoes with four-inch stiletto heels would complete the outfit, and heavy, almost masklike make-up that emphasised her full red lips and huge green eyes. She would stand before Jim as they were getting ready, waiting for his approval, and he would tell her that she looked almost perfect – there was just one thing missing. He'd take a length of fine silk rope and tie her hands tightly behind her body, and she'd know better than to protest. He'd drape a macintosh around her, so her bound hands could not be seen, as they head out to meet me.

I'd be waiting for them at the haunt I'd named, a West End restaurant which has a members' bar that offers utter discretion and seclusion for everyone from businessmen like myself to sports stars who do not want to be disturbed while they eat. Drinking at the bar, I'd smile warmly as I saw them approaching. The waiter would show us to our table, and – as time stands still for a moment – take Gemma's coat. If he's confused by the sight of her tied wrists, he'd say nothing. I'd know it was not all he would be seeing before the night was out.

When he takes our order, I ask for a plate of asparagus for Gemma. Jim and I would be chatting away nonchalantly, as if it weren't at all unusual that this young lady had her wrists bound behind her, but all the while Gemma – sworn to silence – would have a self-conscious flush to her cheeks. She'd be in no position to feed herself unless Jim chose to release her hands, and when I ask Jim if I could feed Gemma, I'm invited cordially to go ahead.

'But I wouldn't want to get butter on that beautiful dress of hers,' I venture.

'Unbutton the dress, then. She won't mind,' he assures me.

My smile widens, and I unfasten the top two buttons of her dress, revealing the upper slopes of her gorgeous breasts. Jim has barely touched his own plate of melon and Parma ham, as I offer the asparagus to Gemma's lips. I make her work for every mouthful, and as she reaches forwards, the butter trickling out of the corner of her mouth and down her neck, I find myself wanting to lick the little golden trail away. Of course, I have to open Gemma's dress further, and when the waiter comes back it's to see my mouth on Gemma's neck and her dress unbuttoned practically to her waist, baring her breasts completely. She's sitting with her back to the rest of the diners so no one else can see what's going on, I'm amused to see the waiter's stammering perplexity – and the obvious bulge in Jim's trousers which has been raised by the sight of Gemma sitting half-naked, impassive, while I lick butter off her skin.

We skip the main course and go straight on to dessert. Both Jim and I are anxious to take Gemma home and use her beautiful body. Jim orders Gemma to spread her legs widely, and I can see his large hand, largely hidden by the crisp white tablecloth, moving between them. When the waiter comes to collect our plates, he's confronted by the sight of Gemma biting her lip as she struggles not to make any sound which would alert our fellow diners to what's happening, while the movements of George's hand make it perfectly clear that he's masturbating Gemma beneath the table. I throw enough money on to the table to pay the bill plus twenty per cent, for what the waiter's discretion has added to the scene, and we leave, Gemma's coat once more loosely draped around her shoulders, offering the odd glimpse of her breasts as she walks.

This kind of subtle stuff is the most powerful to me, the insinuation of sex, and of having someone where I want them. Once outside, I hand Jim my keys as our feet crunch across the gravel car park, and Jim drives us back to my home. As he drives, I'd treat him to a beautiful sight in the rear-view mirror: Gemma, with her dress now completely unfastened and raised so that her naked bottom is against the car's leather upholstery. My flies are undone and, as her husband watches, Gemma ducks her head and takes the head of my penis between her lips. She is an expert when it comes to sucking cock, and soon she has swallowed my entire length. As Jim pulls up in the drive of my house, he glances in the mirror once more to see Gemma licking my come off her lips and me tucking my wilting cock back into my trousers. Once inside the house, Gemma's ordered to strip down to her stockings and suspenders and prostrate herself on the deep-pile carpet of my lounge. She'd look so vulnerable as she hurried to obey – kneeling on all fours, head down, knowing she was not allowed to look at us without permission.

'You have her well trained, Jim,' I say casually, 'but how does she respond to punishment? I'd put down fifty on her rising to the challenge.'

'I'd be robbing you. Why don't you find out?' Jim replies, both of us knowing how humiliating it must be for Gemma to be discussed as though she was not in the room.

'I'd love to,' I say, unbuckling my belt and removing it from the loops in my trousers. Coiling the buckle end around my hand, I'd flex the thick leather thoughtfully and look sternly at Gemma.

'Open your legs wider, slut,' I'd order, and she'd do as she was told without flinching, though knowing that we're now presented with a breathtaking view of the pert pouch of her fanny and the dark pucker of her asshole.

Next my belt whistles past my ear, to land with a loud crack on the cheeks of her bum. Gemma yelps, but holds her position, and I smile at Jim, acknowledging that he's made a fine match. Again and again I bring the belt down on her taut buttocks, raising thick, red stripes that Jim runs his fingers over admiringly. Gemma cries out at every stroke, but does not lift her head, her cries changing to gentle sobbing as I aim the belt lower, catching the crease at the top of her thighs. When I order her to thrust her pelvis towards me, she does so without demur, even though there's now more chance that the belt will strike her sex lips. I can see that Jim is beginning to get impatient for a more active part, and at least because of that I might be wearing out my welcome with his wife. By now, Gemma's ass is a mass of reddish-purple weals, and tears are running down her pretty face, ruining her carefully applied make-up, but I can clearly see a snail-trail of glistening juice on her inner thighs, showing just how turned on she is by what has been done to her. I finish her punishment with a couple of strokes that lash viciously round her thighs, the very tip of the belt catching her pussy lips and causing her to shriek in surprise. In contrast, I bend forward and run my hand tenderly through her now-damp hair. We spend the next hour taking it in turns to fuck Gemma, both of us taking her from behind so that we can savour the sensation of the heat radiating from her heavily welted backside as we thrust into her.

* * *

I dream of captivating a woman and training her to become my submissive slave. I would have control over many aspects of her life, such as what she wears and when she uses the toilet. It would really turn me on to see her asking for permission to pee, knowing that I will be watching her when she does. I'd also gradually train her to offer her body to other men, and to respond to their caresses while in my presence. There could be no sweeter sight than to see her crawling towards me, naked, with the whip I am about to use on her beautiful backside coiled loosely around her neck.

* * *

I imagine I am a dominant master who has taken pleasure over the years in finding suitably submissive females and training them to become obedient, willing slaves. For the last six months, I have been training two girls, Trixi and Trina, and I have just reached the point at which I'm satisfied with their progress and want to turn my attention to someone new when a friend of mine, Hugh, contact me. Hugh is organising an event at his large house on the fringes of Epping Forest, and is interested to know whether I would like the chance to put my two slaves through their paces before a selection of interested parties. Trixi and Trina have always known that one day they would be passed on to someone else, and so when I tell them they would be taking a trip out to Essex where they would have to perform before potential new masters, they accept the fact without question. I take them dressed in nothing more than simple shift dresses, with nothing underneath, and around their necks I strap the wide silver collars which indicated my mastery of the pair. When I talked at length to Hugh about the procedure for the evening, he had told me that I was the only person who would be taking a brace of slaves, and that they would be the last item on the evening's agenda. I knew then that I would be providing the highlight of the night's entertainment, and felt a glow of self-satisfaction, generated by the knowledge that I had trained Trixi and Trina to the highest standards. The assembled guests, I am sure, will receive a rare treat when the two girls are shown off.

There are four other slaves on the bill, two male and two female, and I watch with interest as they are displayed. I'm not in the market for a trained slave – as I have said, I much prefer to take an innocent in these matters and instruct her in the ways of submission myself – but if I were, I'd be more than happy with the performance of a small-breasted redhead called Gina, who takes a dozen strokes of the two-tailed tawse without flinching, before taking the whole length of her would-be master's seven-inch cock down her slender throat. Trixi and Trina have been kept chained by their ankles to a thick wooden post in an anteroom, and when I am asked to fetch them, I rise to my feet and make a small bow to Hugh before leaving the room. Heads turn on my return, eager for a first glimpse of the two girls. Though Trixi is of oriental extraction and Trina a fair-skinned brunette, I have had their hair cropped in the same identical severe style, to show their bone structure to best effect, and they are made up to achieve a masklike effect, rendering them more alike than different. The simple dresses they wear indicate the curves of their bodies without revealing too much, arousing the curiosity of the waiting audience.

I have them stand side by side on the raised dais at one end of the imposing room, heads bowed submissively. 'Gentlemen, may I present Trixi and Trina,' I say. 'I can guarantee the utmost obedience of both of them, as I shall demonstrate.' My voice is icy as I give the first order. 'Strip, the pair of you.' As if choreographed, the girls take hold of the hems of their dresses and raise them over their heads in a single fluid movement. There are appreciative murmurs at the sight of their naked bodies. Each girl wears a gold ring through each nipple, and further rings in her labia and clitoris; to show the latter to best effect, I ordered the two to stand with their legs a foot apart. As you would expect, they are expected to keep their bodies free of hair at all times, and the rings could be seen glinting in the folds of their shaven pussies.

'Assume the display position,' I tell them. Again in perfect harmony, they drop to the ground, kneeling up with their thighs splayed and their bejeweled cunts exposed, their hands linked on top of their heads, lifting and tautening their breasts. Their chests are the one area where the two girls really differ; Trina has large, round breasts which are surprisingly firm given their size, whereas Trixi has the smallest breasts I have ever seen, little more than pads of flesh crowned with large, dark areolae. However, I must admit that I find Trixi's form the more arousing of the two, and I love to caress those tiny swellings with my hands flat to her chest, so that her pierced nipples peep out from between my spread fingers. I can hear the assembled guests muttering amongst themselves, and decide to move on to the next position. 'Display yourselves from behind,' I tell them, and they hurry to obey. Now they are standing with their backs to the audience, bent over at the waist and with their legs wide apart. This position was designed to show off their assholes as well as their denuded pussies, but to give an even better view, they are required to pull their bum cheeks apart with their hands. When I first told the girls that these display positions were a required part of their training, their natural shame overcame them and they were mortified at the thought of anyone being able to see the most intimate parts of their bodies. Now, however, they assume the positions without a second's thought.

'Can we touch?' A grey-haired man who must have been well into his sixties asked eagerly. I looked across at Hugh, who nodded assent. 'Please, gentlemen, be my guests,' I said. That was the signal for the half a dozen or so men to rise from their seats and step up on to the dais. One by one, they run their hands over the bodies of my two slaves as the girls try their hardest not to move or make a sound – both of which they know to be punishable offences. However, it must be difficult for them as cunning fingers stroked their breasts and pinch their nipples, or delve between their legs to insinuate themselves into their moistening vaginas.

Most of the guests take the opportunity to pass comments of the crudest and most uncomplimentary nature on the slaves' physical attributes. One dark-skinned, balding man ran his hands over Trixi's torso and muttered, 'Hasn't got much in the way of tits, has she?'

'You wouldn't believe how sensitive they are, though,' I point out. 'Go on, see for yourself.' I watch as the man takes hold of the ring in one of Trixi's stiff little nipples and tugs it to a degree which must be distressing for my slave. Despite all the warnings I have given her, she cannot prevent herself from letting out a moan which indicates that, far from being in pain, she's becoming aroused by the man's cruel actions. A smile flits across his face as he realises that I have been telling the truth. I have known Trixi to come simply from having those tiny teats pulled and tormented, but I'm sure that if he's interested in acquiring her, he'll find that out for himself. The grey-haired master who first expressed a desire to touch the slaves was running his finger down the crease between Trina's bum cheeks. The tautly stretched skin between her pussy and anus is one of the most sensitive spots on her body, and I can see she is doing her best not to betray the reaction his touch is causing. He takes his index finger and, without even bothering to moisten it with her juices or his saliva, thrusts it roughly into her dusky rosebud. She flinches, and I realise he is doing his best to increase any punishment she will receive as part of the evening's entertainment.

'Isn't it time you showed us how much punishment they can take?' one of the other men asks, and the others hurry to agree with him. I can see more than one pair of trousers is tented with a partial erection, and know they are eager to move on to the climax of the performance. 'Very well,' I say. There is a big iron hook hanging from the ceiling, and I intend to put it to good use. I have brought a selection of restraints and implements of punishment, not knowing exactly what Hugh and his circle were expecting to see, and now I begin to make use of them. I order the slaves to stand upright and put their hands together in front of them, then I cuff each girl's wrists together using padded leather cuffs. Then I tell them to stand beneath the hook, their bodies pressed together. Using a length of chain, I secure the two of them to the hook in the ceiling, their arms above their heads. Trixi, being the smaller of the two, is standing on tiptoes, and both girls' bodies are straining in position. Finally, I wind a long leather strap around them, securing them together at the waist. It's a stunningly erotic sight to see them bound like that, Trina's big breasts squashed against Trixi's flat chest and their pubic bones pressing together.

'The soft cat first, then the bullwhip,' I announce, picking up the first of the two instruments. The suede cat, with its short, soft tails, is one of my favourite toys, ideal for softening up a slave in preparation for a more thorough whipping. I play it lightly over the girls' bound bodies, concentrating on their fleshy bum cheeks and the backs of their thighs. They are soon moaning as the suede thongs land on their skin, and when I curl it around so that it lands on the sensitive pout of Trixi's pussy, there is a little yelp of anguish from her and a purr of appreciation from the audience. I know they want to see the girls take a severe punishment, and that is why I have brought the bullwhip. This is not an instrument to be taken lightly; in the wrong hands it could cause severe injury. There is absolute silence in the room as I lay the whip on with all the skill I possess, lashing it down on the girls' buttocks and watching the livid welts that spring up where it lands. The moans change to shrieks and sobs, and the two slaves twist in their bonds, seeking to escape from the cruel cuts of the whip but knowing they're unable to. Cocks are being stroked at the sight of the girls' punished bodies rubbing together, and at least one of the men there has already climaxed. Finally, I unfasten the leather strap which ties the two together and order the lithe Trixi to wrap her legs around Trina's waist and grind her pubis against the other girl until the stimulation brings them both to come. The audience breaks into spontaneous applause as I unchain my slaves and help them down from the dais. Delighted by their performance, I take them back stage where I administer palliative oils and lotions to their poor, bruised, sinewy bodies, and field several approaches offering them a new home, making arrangements to discuss these offers at a later date.

* * *

I once heard a saying that you know you really care about someone when you fantasise about going round a supermarket or a home improvement store with them! Well, I've often had a fantasy about just that, but with a difference. I'd like to take my lover around one of those giant out-of-town supermarkets, pushing a trolley around like any other couple but with a few additions only her and I know about.

We'd start by getting ready at home. Saturday morning, the busiest time when the harassed and hard-working shoppers, who've been in the office all week, come out to buy their groceries. We'd wake up, and make sure, even if we were still dead sleepy, to have sex first, if only to take off the immediate pressure of the very horny things we were going to go on and do! After a lazy, straightforward fuck, a shower, and some breakfast to make sure our stomachs weren't distracting us, we'd get ready. As for myself, under comfortable outer clothes – jeans and a sweater – I'd strap my cock and balls into a tight harness that bound my scrotum and looped around my penis, lifting both forward and keeping my shaft bent so that it would strain deliciously against the rough straps as it stiffened. I'd leave my nipples unstimulated as I'm going to do the driving and I don't want to cause accidents! I have a small ring in my left anyway, and that would be enough to provide a little stimulation as it rubbed inside my clothes. Then, I'd get my girlfriend ready. I'd gather up her small selection of dildos, and present them for her to pick one, knowing that, if later events get a bit too much for her to bear when we're out among polite company, it'll be all the more delicious for having herself partly to blame as well as me. A practical girl

139

at heart, she picks a smallish, flexible number which is gnarled and knobbled around the middle.

She sits on the bed with her hands on her head as I bind her pert breasts with a cat's cradle of chains, the links small enough to feel smooth overall, and light, but cold and pinching enough to cause just a little discomfort. Her tits bound and framed for me, I tie a small length of shiny gift tape around each erect, red-brown nipple, held in place by the ring in each, giftwrapping them for me, and keeping her in constant uplifted stimulation. Next, I lace her into a small waspy corset that makes her catch her breath slightly and sit demurely erect. She rolls over on the bed, spreads her legs and the fun really begins as I squirt a little Liquid Silk on her anal bud, working it around until my finger slips in easily. Her passage is pleasingly empty and I ease a solid rubber plug into her asshole – one with a small nub on top, tapering into a waist around which her ring clamps, with a widened base beneath that to stop it disappearing inside. She moans as she pushes her ass towards me and her ring out to take it in. Then, moving on to her back and spreading her legs, she gestures for me to fill her with the dildo. I slide it in slowly as she tips her head back and opens herself to it.

I twist myself around until my bound cock and balls are over her face and I go down on her, teasing out her clit from its hood, running my tongue back and forth until it aches, all the while easing the dildo in and out of her cunt. Meanwhile, she licks around the straps and my bound cock, teasing my cockhead with her tongue until it's torment. I think that in revenge I'll get her close to coming and then stop, laughing at her petulance when it's done. But when the moment comes I'm a big softie, and let her steal an orgasm despite my own torture. After she's shuddered to a relaxed halt, I'm pleased to see she's covered in a new sheen of sweat already. Then it's up, no time to recover, and she's strapped and buckled around the pelvis to hold the dildo and the plug in place, along with a new addition: a ribbed butterfly pad which tickles her clit. She runs her hands along the edge of the dressing table, bends over it a little and pushes out her bum for a few slaps from my palm, which warm and redden it enough to take six swift swishes from our light, whippy cane. Welts appear in a wide, barred-gate style – I've placed them well. Her head droops submissively and the sight of her burning-assed shame and fearful anticipation is enough to have my cock pressing painfully hard against its harness until I want to bend over myself to ease the pressure. Her juices are appearing around the edges of the creaky leather strapped tight against her cunt and into her ass, softening it up. I had known she'd wanted her ass warmed with a few strokes so that later she could feel its soft bruisedness, like a peach, as it pressed into the car seat, adding to her welter of sensation. Hence the matter-of-fact nature of their delivery. Usually we'd make a bit more of the shame and anticipation inherent in tools once used as discipline for real, than that.

And so to the supermarket, a deliciously torment-ing drive. She's dressed in suspenders (the belt stretched over her buckles and straps), over which there's a sheath skirt. A high, turtle-necked sweater covers the small metal collar from which a thin, strong chain runs down through her cleavage to loop under her cunt and ass and fasten at the nape of her neck. She's wearing a waisted jacket which covers the odd lines around her chest and hips. One sleeve covers the handcuffs that manacle one wrist to the supermarket trolley, its other cuff hidden by my jacket thrown over the handle. In her state of constant stimulation, she can but totter on her four-inch stilettos. As we wheel our trolley sedately around the aisles like any other couple in the store that morning, no one – or indeed very few – would be able to detect what was going on between us. I contrive to plonk the heaviest – and most unnecessarily heavy – bags of frozen food into the trolley, along with two gallon-jugs of milk, running the girlfriend ragged, her effortful movements causing her tied tits, caned ass and teased cunt to rub relentlessly in never-ending arousal. Eventually, she stands recovering at the checkout as I load the bags from the conveyor belt, and hand over my credit card. But her ordeal isn't over yet. Tottering on her heels, I make her carry the bags across the car park to the car, three large paper bags held in front of her, their weight pushing her bound tits into her body. She's breaking a sweat. Eventually we reach the car. Oops! I can't find my keys! Oh, there they are. Needless to say, we drive back to my apartment, rip and peel the clothes and straps from each other, and fuck like hell as quickly as we can, digging our nails into each other's skin as the groceries defrost in the trunk of the car.

* * *

The Landlord Calls

Kerry Crossland was forty-two years old and she lived with her daughter-in-law Deborah, who was twenty years younger. Both of them were widowed early. Kerry worked in a local supermarket and Deborah was a cleaner.

'How far are you behind on the rent Kerry?'

The older woman was in debt to the landlord for quite a lot more than she could afford and Debbie was shocked.

'I can pay it with the insurance money,' the younger girl offered. 'No love, it's my problem and I will have to sort it.'

Kerry Crossland was into gambling and had lost a lot of money, if it hadn't been for Deborah there would have been no money for food either.

The dreaded knock came to the door. It was Mr Rostron, the man who owned the house.

'Please come in Mr Rostron,' Kerry asked him.

'I don't have a lot of time Mrs Crossland. I will come to the point, you have ten days to leave this house.'

'But where can I go? I have nothing!'

'I am afraid that is your problem and not mine. My problem is getting money out of you.'

'Please give me a month, if I can't pay I will leave.'

'I have given you more than enough time, I am not made of money.'

'I know that Mr Rostron. I need one big win. I know this horse will win.'

'Nothing is certain, Mrs Crossland.'

'Just one month, I can do it honest.'

'I will give you the month, then I will find some other way of getting the money from you.'

When Mr Rostron had left, Deborah asked, 'What will you use for money to put on the horse?'

'I don't know love, but this one is a dead cert, I know it.'

Debbie opened her purse and took out what notes she had. 'There is sixty here Mum, make it good!' She always called her 'Mum' when she was worried.

Kerry had thirty pounds in her pocket and after a look around the house she had scraped up one hundred pounds.

'It won, Debbie. It won at forty-to-one!'

She gave her daughter-in-law fifteen hundred pounds and stuffed the rest in her pocket. The month was up and Mr Rostron was at the door, Deborah was out at work.

'Do you have the money?' He asked.

'Look Mr Rostron, I have no money.'

'You now have one week, seven days and you are out.'

'Please, there has to be another way.'

'Only one way and that is to let me thrash your bottom whenever I want to!'

Kerry had wondered what he meant on his last visit and she was now finding out about her landlord.

'Mr Rostron, you are going too far. I can't allow something of that nature.'

'I will be back in two days at the same time, you will either pay what is due or you will leave my house, or you will let me thrash your bottom.'

'Get out you perverted bastard, I'll find your fucking money somehow.'

Friday came and she was alone once more. 'Where is the money Mrs Crossland?'

'I have none,' she told him, looking sad.

'You had better pack, I want you out of here in twenty-four hours.'

'Wait a minute, you offered me another choice?'

'Yes I did, but you threw me out of my own house and called me a perverted bastard. Twenty-four hours Mrs Crossland, not an hour more.'

Rostron left but was back ten minutes later, Kerry had been sobbing. 'Well Mrs Crossland, you can take up my offer but I promise you a real good thrashing if you accept.'

'Oh God, Mr Rostron, I promise you that I will take what is coming to me. I will do what you say.'

'Anything I say?'

'Whatever, Mr Rostron. You have my word.'

'I will be back at two o'clock this afternoon to see to it.'

'Thank you, you won't regret it!'

'I hope not, but just to show willing, you can bend over the arm of the sofa.'

Kerry bent over as she was told, she was wearing red trousers and he gave the bending bottom four smacks. These were not hard nor were they too light.

'Yes, you show promise, Mrs Crossland. Expect me at two this afternoon. Please wear something a little more daring!'

When he had gone Kerry went into the bathroom and took down her trousers. The little tight briefs followed and she looked in the full-length mirror at her bottom. There was not a lot to see, only a slight pinkness on each cheek where his hand had landed. She took a bath and after drying she put on a pair of yellow panties and bra to match. This was topped off with her best skirt and blouse.

The bell rang, it was five minutes to the appointed hour. Mr Rostron was standing on the step. There was a carrier bag in his hand and a smile on his face.

'Please come in Mr Rostron.'

'Very kind of you,' he told her looking her up and down. 'You have done yourself proud in that attire.'

'Thank you. Can I get you a drink or something?'

'No. Just bring one of the dining chairs over.'

When the chair was positioned to his liking, Mr Rostron sat on it and passed Kerry the carrier bag he had brought with him. She looked inisde. It was a beautiful pair of slippers.

'Try them on Mrs Crossland, they are for you.'

The slippers were a perfect fit, she wondered why he had done this.

'Please pass me one and lie across my lap.'

Now she knew why he had bought her the slippers. As she lay down where he wanted her he lifted up her skirt and saw the tight yellow panties.

'Very nice, Mrs Crossland.'

He spanked these by hand a good number of times then used one of the slippers which she had passed him. The landlord gave her twenty more with this and let her up.

'I will be back tomorrow, same place, same time.'

'But I did as you wanted, I let you spank me.'

'You let me tap your bottom a few times. Every day we will go a little harder and you will be expected to help a little more.'

The next day she was waiting in a pair of tight shorts and a T-shirt. 'Very nice yet again,' he told her, handing her a strap.

'Now just a minute, Mr Rostron.'

'No you wait a minute, I said each day will be more painful. Now do you keep your word or do you get the fuck out of my house?' She was shocked by his language as if she had never used it before, she knew he was right, he had put up with so much from her.

'Shorts off, please.'

'Oh God.'

'Yes, I spank knickers, Mrs Crossland.'

'Of course she had no choice other than to obey, she unbuttoned the shorts and pulled them down her legs. What was the fuss? He had spanked her on her panties yesterday. The knickers were flesh-coloured and these got thirty smacks with the strap.

'Please be here tomorrow at the same time, I have something else for you.'

The next visit he brought a flat wooden paddle with him and she was over his knee as soon as it had been unwrapped. It cracked on her pale green panties two dozen times then he let her up.

'I will see you tomorrow Mrs Crossland, same time.'

Saturday was the cane, he made her touch her toes for this and on lifting her skirt, he gave her ten stingers.

On the Sunday she was left alone but Monday he had her over his lap in her best blue knickers. These were soundly spanked, as was the flesh just below each leg of them.

'Now Mrs Crossland, as this is your second week I am going to bare this . . .'

'You are fuck!' she replied, grabbing her panties to prevent him removing them.

'They come down, or you leave the house. You gave me your word.'

'Oh Jesus, I suppose you had better get them off then, you dirty pervert.' She moved her hands down by her sides and felt him pulling her knickers down. His hand cracked down on the bare flesh of her bottom twenty times then made her open her parcel while remaining in position. It was a clothes brush with a large flat back and long handle.

'Oh no, please Mr Rostron, this will sting.'

'It is meant to, stay still until it is all over, you can cry if you feel the need.'

She not only cried, she yelled, as all ten whacks landed on the cheeks of her perfectly formed bottom.

On the Tuesday he brought a thick leather belt. 'Skirt and panties off right away Mrs Crossland, and bend right over the arm of the chair.'

She was in position, bare ass uppermost. He used the belt twenty times. On the Wednesday it was a short riding crop, and after lashing her bum twenty times he groped at her breasts through the thin blouse.

'Tomorrow you will not wear a bra, please.'

He was back at his normal time the following day and a large whip had been wrapped up for her to open.

'Oh Jesus, not this, please.'

'Over the rear of the sofa now,' he told her, as she was down to her white blouse only. He could tell that she had obeyed his instruction from the day before as her huge nipples were protruding through the silky material.

He only lashed her ten times, before feeling her breasts, letting his thumb gently stroke each nipple in turn.

'I am going to use this item each day and on each visit the pain will be a little bit harder.'

On the Friday there was of course no present as she had left the whip out ready for him to use. He had her down to her blouse and over his knees for a lengthy tanning before using the whip once more as she bent over the sofa.

Of course he felt her breasts again, tweaking the swollen nipples. 'Oh God,' she asked, 'How much more of this do I have to go through?'

'I will let you know when I am ready.'

'Would you please leave it over the weekend? My daughter-in-law will be here as it is her weekend off.'

'As you both live here I would like her to share your punishment.'

'You can't; she pays her share but I never give it to you.'

'In that case when I come tomorrow I would like to see her here so that she can witness what happens to you.'

Bending her over the settee once more he lashed her bottom with the cane five times then asked her, 'Do you want five more or will you take off the blouse?'

'You take it off, Mr Rostron,' she told him, 'you'll possibly get more kicks out of it that way.'

He wasted no time, and poor Kerry was soon naked in his sight and to his hands.

'Now please relax, Mrs Crossland.'

Picking up the whip he began to stroke her bush with it and eventually got eight inches of it inside her pussy from behind. She was relaxed at first but began to relax even more when the thick handle was buried deep inside her.

It took a while for her to come and when she had, Mr Rostron left her alone.

Kerry Crossland was over the bath gently washing her rear when her daughter-in-law Deborah came in. Kerry had just masturbated for the second time after Rostron's visit. Deborah was shocked to see her bottom in the state it was in, and Kerry had to tell her everything.

'And how long will the two of you be doing this?'

'Until I pay him whatever is due on the rent, but I think he is enjoying it too much to pack it in too early.'

'Well, you got yourself into a real mess, you and your stupid horses!'

'Not just me Debbie; he wants you to be with me tomorrow. He wants you to watch everything that he does to me. I think he is hoping to get you into the same thing as soon as he can.'

'He can sod off – there is no way I will be part of this.'

'What will you do tomorrow when he gets here?'

'I will stay in my bedroom.'

'Oh please Debbie, you must help me, he only wants you to watch me get a thrashing. Surely you can do this for me?'

'Not on your life Mum, you dug yourself into this mess, you can dig your bloody self out of it.'

Rostron was there dead on two o'clock the following day. 'What shall we use today before we start on the whip?' he asked, seeing all the presents he had brought her laid out as he had asked.

'Oh please Mr Rostron, tell me how much I owe you and I will see if I can get it together, I can't take too much more of this.'

'If you want a statement of accounts you can have one at the end of this session.'

'Oh no, you mean I have to suffer some more?'

'Surely it has not all been pain, and where is that lovely daughter-in-law of yours?'

'I sent her out, there is no need for her to be subjected to all this.'

'Okay then, as you have failed to do as you were informed you alone must take more than I planned to give you.'

Kerry began to sob.

Get everything off except your knickers. You will be thrashed by everything in this room before I use the whip.'

'Oh please Mr Rostron – not like this, I beg of you?'

'The money earned up to now can be taken away just as easy as it was added.' Kerry knew that she was beaten whichever way she went. Her blouse came off and the man's eyes went immediately to the two mounds which he loved so much, his hands weren't far behind, caressing and tweaking. Rostron didn't go at it like a bull in a china shop like her ex-husband used to do. The fingers were gentle, his hands warm on her breasts. She thought that the more she kept him up there he might forget what he had originally come in for. Besides, she loved what he was doing to her, the fingers just lightly touching her protruding nipples. Would he use his lips, his tongue? She hoped so.

Rostron's hands slid slowly down her back and rested on her bottom. He was stroking the two well-punished cheeks which he so much loved to chastise.

One hand went to the zipper on her skirt and pulled it down as the other continued the gentle movements over her panties. The skirt dropped down her legs to form a puddle at her feet and now, as she had been ordered, she was naked down to her panties.

The hand stopped the gentle caressing and he pulled her arm so that as he sat down Kerry fell immediately into position.

'Oh please, I thought for once you were going to forget this part of things.'

'You have to be joking!' he told her as he raised his hand and brought it down on to her pretty pink knickers. After a good twenty spanks with his hand, followed by the same with the clothes brush he picked up the razor strop, the slipper, and finally, on removing her panties, he went back to using his hand.

'Over the back of the settee now Kerry – you know the position.' She did, and over she went, with legs open. She could sense him behind her with cane and whip, which he would soon be using on her reddened ass, as she was pushing it up as much as she could. She gulped as she thought of just what that whip could do, in more areas than one.

The cane cracked down four times then it was four with the whip. She screamed as each one of these landed on her naked flesh.

'Now, Kerry my dear, little non-payer of rent, do you want the handle?'

'If you say so, Mr Rostron.'

'Are you ready for it?'

'Yes, oh God, yes.'

The handle of the whip, five inches in diameter in the shape of a fully erect penis was slowly, inch by inch, sliding into her warm, moist pussy. It was all the way inside her now as far as it would go. Rostron was pulling it out a little then pushing it back again as if it was his penis he was using.

Kerry was writhing and panting to feel as much of this foreign object as she could.

'I'm coming, oh God' she shouted. 'Oh Jesus, faster please Mr Rostron' He obliged by twisting, pushing and pulling until she screamed to one hell of a climax.

'Mr Rostron, this bit is marvellous, couldn't we do without the lead-up?'

'It wouldn't be anywhere near as good without the spanking side, Kerry.'

'Oh I don't know,' she told him, wiping the sweat from her face and looking for her knickers.

'Wait a minute Kerry, you can have your daughter-in-law's share as well. Back over please.'

Kerry did as she was told and as she bent, there was a huge grin on her face. The whip handle was in about an inch when the door opened and a voice stated, 'I can take my own medicine, if neither of you mind.'

Deborah was dressed in a pair of yellow lace panties and nothing else. These were damp at the crotch and if anyone had taken the time to smell at this item or at her fingers they would have known how long she had been listening at the door, also just what those fingers had been doing.

'So,' said old man Rostron, 'You lied to me.'

'Sorry Mr Rostron,' both females said as one.

'You will be. Come over my lap, young woman.'

'I was hoping just for the final part, but I suppose that is out of the question,' Deborah told him, while going over Rostron's lap, and preparing her bottom for a thrashing.

'Very much so I'm afraid.'

The younger girl took the thrashing her mother-in-law had been given, and when the cane and whip had been used for what he wanted the whip was then used for what Deborah so much wanted and needed. Her own orgasm was terrific. She had never felt this way before, and when the whip handle was removed, she was still oozing.

'Now, for your lies, you can both bend over side by side.'

The two bottoms were caned together. They got six each, and while they were in position he helped them to spread their legs. Taking Deborah first, he forced the whip handle once more inside her lovely golden quim. She screamed to a second fulfilment before Kerry got her share. It took the older woman longer to come than the daughter-in-law, as she knew how to hold back.

'You have nearly finished your payments ladies. There is just one more thing I would like to put inside your love slots.'

'I thought you would never stop with the whip and give us what we need.' He gave both of them his full erect penis and had them crying for joy as he showed them the rent statement, which read, 'Paid in full.'

'You both know what to expect if you get behind with the rent again,' he told them.'

'Yes, Mr Rostron, we sure know what to expect.' Kerry told him, and Deborah nodded.

I am going abroad for a month and when I return I want to see marks on those bottoms. If there isn't enough punishment I will give both of you what you require.'

When he had gone Kerry opened her bank book and looked at the amount of money she had in it.'

'You had more than enough to buy the house many times over with your money. Why not buy the house and stop all this thrashing?' Deborah asked.

'Don't ask stupid questions girl,' Kerry told her, putting on her coat.

'Where are you off to Mum?'

'I owe money to a couple of bookies, see you later.'

'Jesus,' said Deborah, looking at the whip hanging out of herself. 'Come home soon, Mr Rostron.' She knew that soon she would be under the hands and anything else of him. 'I know you have more than one way to collect your rent, I just know you have.'

* * *

Here's a story based on a fantasy around the deliciously un-PC experiences my brother and I, I think, both wish we could have after years as co-directors of the family firm!

All the other girls told me when I joined that the bosses could be very generous with their Christmas bonuses – as long as you were prepared to meet their demands. I wondered what they meant but I did not think too much about it, partly because the boss in my old job would not have given a bonus if it had slapped him in the face.

I found out exactly what was involved last week of November, when we were told we would be seeing the bosses individually to decide the size of our bonus. There are five girls in the department I work for, and as the newest member of staff, I was the last one to be seen on the Friday. The company is run by two brothers, both in their early sixties. You have to admire them as they built it up from nothing, but they have a reputation among their competitors for being old-fashioned in their ways. For instance, they like female staff members to wear skirts, rather than trousers and, though my legs are my best feature, I did have a problem with that particular requirement. I was still nervous and as I waited to see them the other girls in the department would tell what the interview entailed, and I couldn't help but wonder if they were hiding something. I soon found out, as I knocked on the door of the office, with its beautiful wood and thick carpet the colour of blackberries. The Smith brothers were sitting together behind a long desk. They smiled benevolently at me and asked me to sit down, but that air of good humour soon vanished as they outlined what was required of me.

'The system here is a little old-fashioned, and we're proud of it,' the older Mr Smith said. He was the better-looking of the two, having retained a full head of white hair where his brother's had receded more. 'We firmly believe in rewarding success and punishing failure.' At the word 'punish' I must have looked startled, because the younger Mr Smith chipped in, 'Don't worry, Julie, you haven't failed. In fact, we are very pleased with how well you have performed since you arrived here, and the only question we need to answer is how large a bonus we shall be giving you. You can help us to determine that by removing your jacket and blouse.'

I thought they were joking at first, and stared at them blankly. The older Mr Smith said quite sternly, 'Come now, Julie, it's not much to ask, is it?' I supposed he had a point; after all, to sit in front of these two old men in my bra was not so difficult. After all, I would have shown them more if I had been sitting on the beach in my bikini, so I shrugged off my navy blue jacket and placed it over the back of the chair. My white blouse followed it, the brothers' expressions becoming more interested with every button I undid.

'There, that wasn't so painful, was it?' asked the older Mr Smith. I glanced down briefly at my breasts, cradled in the plain white cotton bra, and shook my head briefly.

'So I take it you won't object if we ask you to remove your skirt and tights – or are they stockings?' his brother said quickly, with what I detected was a hopeful note in his voice.

'They're tights,' I replied, then paused for a long, long moment before adding, 'and no, I won't object.' I know I should really have called a halt to proceedings at that point, but I was being driven by other considerations. While money is not exactly a problem for me and my husband, a bigger bonus would help us to have a more comfortable Christmas. I stood up, and unfastened my skirt before dropping it and adding it to the growing pile of clothes beside the chair. When I took off my sensible tights I was surprised that the younger Mr Smith asked that I hand them to him. He sniffed at the gusset, before opening a drawer in his desk and slipping them inside. I thought I got a brief glimpse of stocking, and something white and lacy, before he shut it again, but I could not be sure.

'Very nice,' the older Mr Smith said. 'How do you keep your body in such good trim, Julie? Do you go to the gym, like some of the other girls, or burn off the calories fucking your husband?' I did not know how to respond to such a question, and tried to stammer an answer like a rabbit trapped in headlights, and realised for the first time that I might be in a situation I couldn't easily get out of.

This was proved by the older Mr Smith's words. 'Your bra, Julie. Take that off.' If I did this, there was no going back. I would be asked to answer other rude questions, or show more of my body. I wished one of the others had given me some advice, and that I could have asked them how far they had gone to please our lecherous bosses. But I was on my own, and could only do what my instincts told me. I didn't want to do what they asked, but the alternative was worse. They had talked about punishment, and might not award me the bonus I had already set my heart upon. Or they might have punishment of a physical kind in mind. I could feel welling tears in my eyes as I reached behind and unfastened the bra.

When I dropped it on the desk in front of them, there was silence for a moment. I knew they were both staring at my breasts, and wished I knew what they were thinking. I have always thought they are too small, though my husband, Keith, loves them. At last, the younger Mr Smith said, 'Very nice. Little ones are more sensitive, aren't they, Julie? Do you find that? When your husband pinches them, does the feeling travel to your cunt?' The shock of this kindly looking, white-haired gentleman using such a crude word was like a physical blow, but there was no denying the truth of his question. When Keith plays with my tits I do feel it in my cunt, and he can take me to the brink of orgasm just by nibbling my nipples. I just nodded dumbly, and hoped he would take that as an answer. 'Prove it to me, Julie,' he said. 'Pinch your nipples for me.'

Too dazed to object, I did as he asked, feeling a surge of pure sensation arrowing down to my pussy as I gripped my nipples between thumb and forefinger. I could not prevent a little moan from escaping my lips, and when I looked up, the brothers were watching me with rapt, feral expressions.

'You realise the bonus will go up extensively if you take off your knickers,' the older Mr Smith said. Of course I did; I would have been stupid not to. Everything that had happened until now had been leading up to the moment when I stood before them naked. I gave an involuntary little sob as I pulled down my panties. I had been a virgin when I married, and no one but my husband had ever seen me like this. I was shamefully aware that if the brothers asked to see the panties they would find them wet and infer, correctly, that on some hidden level I was turned on by what was being done to me.

The two old men looked at each other, and me, holding my panties in front of my sex as an ineffectual little shield. 'Would you mind, Julie?' The younger Mr Smith said, holding out his hand to take them from me. Though my reluctance must have been obvious to both of them, I meekly handed them over. This time, he sniffed them extensively, savouring their scent like the bouquet of a fine wine. I began to relax, thinking that this was it and that I could dress and leave with payment secure.

His next words shocked me back to full wariness. 'There's just one last thing,' he said. 'Your annual bonus is performance-related. Did the girls not tell you?' Of course not. They must have known how I would react at the thought of giving my body to lechers, for that was what was being suggested. I wondered how many of them had agreed to the proposal, spurred on as I had been by greed. I could hardly stand the thought of their gnarled, liver-spotted hands pawing my backside and their wizened old cocks entering my cunt, but somehow I found myself saying, 'They didn't tell me but that's not a problem.'

'Good girl,' the older Mr Smith said, moving around the desk towards me. He was unzipping his fly as he came, and as he brought his penis out into the light I could see that it was only partially erect, hanging limply between his fingers. 'Suck,' he urged, and I sank to my knees on that carpet and obediently took the head between my lips. It seemed to take ages for the thing to grow under my ministrations, and all the time I sucked it, I was aware of his brother, standing beside us, wanking his own puny member to full hardness. Neither cock could have been more than five inches long, and in other circumstances I might have compared them to my husband's big, fat prick and laughed, but this was no laughing matter. The fact the two of them had remained fully clothed just emphasised my total nudity, and I felt vulnerable and completely at their mercy. When the older Mr Smith was at last erect, he made me bend over the big wooden desk and spread my legs wide. I felt his brother's elderly fingers reach between my legs, sticking the wetness they found there over the head of my clit. He rubbed me until I was on the brink of orgasm and then, cruelly, he pulled his hand away. While he stood, licking my juices from his fingers, his brother's cock pressed at the entrance to my cunt. I groaned as he eased himself home and began to thrust, feeling the zip on his trousers rasping the delicate flesh of my pussy. He was swift and brutal in his fucking, despite his advanced age, and within a couple of minutes I felt him jerk once, hard, and squirt his come deep inside me.

He pulled out, only for his brother to take his place. As I was fucked for the second time, the older Mr Smith merely wiped his subsiding manhood with a tissue and readjusted his clothing. By now, I was desperate with need, and I found myself begging the younger Mr Smith to make me come. I no longer cared that these men were using me with disdain and, in fact, the thought was only adding to the fire which burned in my belly. His answer was to push me harder against the desk, so that my pubic bone was rubbing along the polished wood. That extra stimulation was just enough to push me over the edge, and I cried out as I came, my pussy spasming around the boss's stubby cock. As the younger Mr S climaxed, too, I knew that I had well and truly earned my bonus. They kept my underwear, of course, but were as good as their word regarding a generous Christmas package!

Male Sexual Fantasy in the 21st Century

THE QUESTIONNAIRE

A. QUESTIONS ABOUT YOU: *What is your age?* 36 years. *Are you single – or in a long-term partnership or marriage?* The latter, as much as anything's ever guaranteed. *Are you: heterosexual, homosexual, or bisexual?* Straight but not blinkered, maybe wonder. Had a couple of gay experiences way back. If it was cold enough . . .

What, if anything, do you find offensive? Please list things – objects, actions or even attitudes – which are to do with sex or which are often associated with sex and which offend you. In photographs, on television or in films: nothing. *In novels:* even less. *In real life:* people who use swastikas and Nazi uniforms to get off in SM games. There's plenty you can do besides. It's said Hitler would've hated it, but you wouldn't be getting your fun that way if it hadn't really happened.

B. ABOUT YOUR SEXUAL FANTASIES *(Definition: What you think about when you think about sex in such a way that you become sexually aroused.):*

How often, on average, do you have sexual fantasies?
Sometimes I think about it all the time, see it
everywhere. Can't get it out of my head however
inappropriate the occasion. Other times I'm really
turned off, brain on a stick, and can't be bothered
with thinking about it at all for a few days.

*Do your fantasies tend to have recurring themes or
subjects? If there are recurring themes or subjects, what
are they?* I suppose it's dominating women, but not
so far as some horrible scene where they're really
hating it. Also being on the receiving end sometimes
so I know how it feels. *Do you have a current favourite
fantasy, or a fantasy that you enjoy more than most?*

- I'm a seventeenth-century English landowner, and
  I catch a local village girl making her way across
  my land. She's bucolically healthy, with long dark
  hair and a well-fed, pneumatic ass and pair of tits.
  She bites her lower lip fearfully as I haul her in her
  diaphanous cambric shift on to my horse. She lies
  across the pommel of my saddle, peachy ass
  upturned. I fasten her arms behind her back with a
  bit of spare rein, and begin to slap her ass because
  I can't resist it, bouncing there before me, softening
  it up. My ancestral pile would have a bunch of old
  priest-holes, heavy iron cuffs and chains, cellars;
  that kind of stuff, left over from the Interregnum,
  and I'd make ample use of these, and wouldn't let
  my servants, male and female, go short of their
  pleasures either. Of course I couldn't really take an
  ugly scene. In fantasy, she'd be ultimately reassured
  that I was going to let her go, or gutsy enough that
  it didn't bother her. Either way she'd be enjoying it.
- Mud, rubber, rain, playfulness outdoors. But
  really, I'd settle for just being liked!

C. ABOUT YOUR SEXUALITY: *Think back to when you were discovering your sexuality, your sexual orientation, and the sexual themes that are now part of your personality. What did you find erotic in those days? What things (for instance films, or books, or items of clothing) or people or experiences were a turn-on?*

When I was younger, older women were something I always found attractive. I suppose it's because I was a fairly sheltered lad who knew mostly older women. I didn't have any sisters, only a couple of female cousins I never saw. I liked their voluptuousness. And maybe a few of them were bored enough to pay me some attention. Mums of friends, teachers, and, back when I was in the fourth form, sixth-form girls who acted like their shit didn't stink.

What would improve your sex life?

- A bit more submission. Complete loss of control, a bit of pain when I'm at the right pitch, rather than humiliation or shame (get quite enough of that in my everyday life). Straitjackets, full enclosure, blindfolds, headphones, with no control over what I listen to – white noise, for example, being vacuum-packed. Domination and submission are two sides of the same coin and it's nice to know how the other half live.
- Women knowing how much they could turn me on with everything but my dick – nipples, perineum, ass especially.
- Not losing my wallet in the playroom like I did the last time I went to a fetish club.
- A vasectomy.

* * *

My mate Jim and I have had some memorable times in the years we have been working together, but the one that sticks in my mind is when we went to do a building job for a bloke in the posh part of town. He had a job in the City which meant he commuted in every day, leaving his wife at home. She was the type who has never done an honest day's work in her life and just lived off his fat salary, and she treated Jim and me the same way she probably treated anyone who came to do any work at that place – like a lower form of life.

It was August, and blisteringly hot, as we started the construction work on the conservatory they wanted. Normally, Jim and I would walk about quite happily stripped to the waist and wearing cut-off denim shorts, but that was not to the liking of Mrs Fortune (or Cynthia, as we were definitely not allowed to call her), and so we sweltered away in T-shirts and jeans while the temperatures climbed into the nineties. Occasionally, she would condescend to bring us a cool drink or ask us if we needed anything, but mostly she would sit around on a sun lounger wearing a tiny bikini, almost as if she wanted us to gawp at her. She seemed to get off on the fact that dirty, common workmen like us could look we were not allowed to touch. Mind you, it seemed like her husband was in the same boat as us. If I told you that her old man was in his fifties while she was a good twenty years younger, I think that will give some idea of what their marriage was like. We picked up the impression that although she had a stunning body, with big tits and a luscious ass, her husband very rarely got his hands on it, the poor sod. As the week went on, and she continued to condescend to us, we decided she needed to be brought down a peg or two. She had had a couple of friends round for lunch on the Friday, and the three of them had gawped and stared at us as we worked away, smoothing concrete into place on the floor of the conservatory. As they pointed and laughed, Jim was harbouring thoughts about pushing her face into the concrete. I had a different kind of humiliation in store for Cynthia. A couple of hours later, I got the chance I had been waiting for. Mrs Fortune was lying on the lounger, fast asleep, the book she had been reading forgotten on the grass. As usual, she was wearing her polka-dot bikini which consisted of little more than a series of minute triangles of fabric. I took my Stanley knife from the tool kit, and crept over to where she was snoring gently. She did not stir as I took hold of the thin strip of fabric between the cup bikini, and sliced it in two. Then I did the same to the halter fastening of the top before turning my attention to the tie sides of her bikini. Satisfied with my handiwork, I quietly coughed in her ear. She jerked awake and looked around her.

'What the hell do you think you're doing, you filthy lecher?' she snapped. 'Spying on a defenceless woman when she's asleep.'

'I wasn't exactly spying,' I replied, trying to keep the smirk from my face. When she had sat up, the bikini top had fallen apart, and she did not seem to realise that I could now see her naked tits with their plump pink nipples.

'What are you staring at?' she asked. 'Just go and get on with your work. I'm going to go and run myself a bath and I don't want to be disturbed. Honestly, I should ring my husband and tell him to sack the pair of you.' 'Yeah, you do that, love,' I said. She rose to her feet in fury, obviously about to say something, then stopped as she felt the scraps of material that had once been her bikini bottom slithering down her legs.

'What the hell?' she exclaimed, glancing down her body. Her hands flew to cover her nipples and pussy, but not before I had got a good look at her cunt. I could not fail to notice that it was considerably darker than the ash-blonde hair on her head. She turned and made a dash for the house, but that was when I realised Jim had played our trump card. He was sitting on the doorstep, waving the key to the back door and grinning his head off. Mrs Fortune looked rapidly from one to the other of us, weighing up the situation and quickly coming to the realisation that Jim and I had the upper hand.

'What are you going to do to me?' she asked anxiously, obviously afraid that we might hurt her. Of course, that was not our intention, but there was no harm in letting her get a little worried.

'Actually, it's what you're going to do to us,' I replied. 'We're sick of the fact that you treat us like something you've scraped off the heel of your shoe, and we're tired of the way you flaunt your body all the time, trying to turn us on.'

'I never . . .' she began, but I had spoken the truth, and she knew it.

'So what you're going to do, Cynthia, is for your rudeness and your snobby ways, begin by giving me and Jim a nice blow job each.'

'You can't expect me to do that,' she said angrily. 'I mean, my husband doesn't expect me to . . .' her voice trailed away as she realised just what she'd started telling us. As I said before, the poor sod. There was the sound of a zip coming down and when Cynthia and I looked round, it was to see Jim holding his cock and giving it a few firm tugs to bring it to full erection. I've seen Jim in football club showers before, so what he was holding was no surprise to me, but Cynthia's mouth was hanging open as she took

165

in the sight of eight inches of hard, pulsating flesh – with a lust, fear and surprise or a combination of the three.

'Come on, wrap those luscious lips of yours around this,' Jim said, with the cocksureness of one who knows when the scales are tipped in his favour. Cynthia glanced at me in mute appeal, but as far as I was concerned, she deserved everything that she had coming to her, and I wanted to savour it. A push in the small of her back sent her to her knees in front of Jim, and when he put the head of his cock to her lips she merely gave a little gasp and took it in her mouth. For the next ten minutes or so, she sucked that huge, solid column of flesh, her lips at their widest around its bulbous head. I could not resist taking my own cock and wanking lazily as I watched Cynthia's dyed blonde hair bobbing up and down frantically. At last, Dave grunted that he was coming, and pulled out of Cynthia's mouth to spray her face and hair with jet after jet of viscous spunk. She used her fingers to wipe the sticky stuff off her skin as best she could.

Now it was my turn, and I was more keen to sample Cynthia's cunt than her mouth. However, I hid one more humiliation planned for her first. I told her to lie down and spread her legs for me. Her eyes widened as I picked up the Stanley knife once more and took one of the mousy curls that covered her mound. 'Don't worry,' I told her, 'I just like to get a better view of what I'm getting into.' I used the knife to hack the curl away. Working quickly, I reduced the forest of hair to nothing more than messy and uneven stubble. As I did, I took every opportunity to dip my fingers into the growing pool of juice at the entrance to her cunt. She tried, unsuccessfully, to stifle a moan as I touched her clit almost absent-mindedly with my finger. I was determined that by the time I had finished this tight-assed bitch would be begging me to fuck her.

At last, I threw the knife to the ground and pulled my jeans and underpants down and off. Pushing Cynthia's legs even further apart, I positioned myself between them and thrust up into her cunt. While I can't match up to Jim in the size department, I know what to do with what I have got, and she was soon whimpering and writhing beneath me as I ground my pelvis hard against hers. Her hot, tight channel clutched convulsively at my cock and I knew she was coming. The spasms were fierce enough to trigger my own orgasm, and I shot my load deep inside her, what I can only describe as the climax of a very good afternoon's work.

Needless to say, Cynthia was as nice as pie towards us for the couple of days that remained until we finished the job. But it just goes to show you should never treat people as though they are beneath you, because the tables might get turned and you might end up beneath them.

* * *

My girlfriend came home one evening to find me half drunk, and sharing a spliff with a guy she'd never seen before. He was big, rough-looking and covered in tattoos. In fact he was Davey, my best mate from way back. He'd looked me up only that morning, ringing the doorbell unannounced, and luckily I had a day off which I was wondering how to spend. I let Davey banish any worthy thoughts I'd had of home improvement. He had, he said, been working in the Gulf for the last six months and, flashing a generous wad of cash, said that he could afford to stand me a few rounds and felt like a few pints himself, making up for lost drinking time having been living in a Muslim country. As we drank, it transpired he'd been doing without something else for six months, too. Knowing how submissive my girlfriend Jackie can be, given half a chance, I thought perhaps I could offer him something he was in need of, in return for all the drinks!

I wasn't wrong about Jackie. When she came in from work, she did me proud, going down on Davey and even letting him slap her ass a few times. I think she was turned on by how rough he looked – tattoos, a dirty-looking tan from working outside, and by how big he was. Then he dropped to his knees, pressing his lips to her pussy and gently kissing her clit. 'Part your legs, babe,' I urged her. 'Give him what he wants.'

She did as I asked, feeling Davey's tongue lapping her cunt honey. She moaned; it might have been a long time since Davey had been with a woman, but he was no novice when it came to licking one out. He seemed to know exactly where to press to give pleasure, his tongue flickering expertly Jackie's prominent clitoris. The stubble on his cheek rasped against her delicate flesh, and she caught hold of his head, pulling his mouth harder on to her sex to bring her to orgasm. It seemed that after all that beer, he was craving a taste of cunt-juice too. She did not care that she had met this man half an hour ago, or, that I had her in that position so I could watch another lick her. All that mattered now was that she was about to come like a train, and held Davey's head in place until the orgasm had finally ebbed away.

Davey asked me if he could spend the rest of the night with Jackie, and of course I agreed. That night he had his first experience in six months of fucking a pussy, and she was more than happy to let him, as was I. He's been a mate for a very long time and I would have let him anyway, without minding, but I was surprised to find, not having thought of myself as a voyeur before, that I was so turned on by watching my girlfriend get fucked by this rough, well-endowed builder-type that I can't wait for a threesome.

* * *

Kim loved hotels, their impersonality, their full service. In fact, she'd probably been dreaming about them. Kim had no idea how long she had slept, or what had woken her. Opening one eye, she saw the sunlight falling across her pillow. It must be around mid-morning. There was a shuffling behind her and what sounded like the small squeak of unoiled machinery, and she knew at once it wasn't the first time she'd heard them – they'd woken her. Blearily, she wondered what – or who – it was. She raised herself on one elbow and turned her head to peer, with lidded eyes from which she brushed her tousled hair, over her shoulder.

Across the room, she saw two figures in check smocks hunched over a metal trolley, its uppermost surface full of plastic bottles and bunches of cloths. She'd never seen such assiduous chambermaids. 'Hey look, excuse me, do you think you could come back in a little while?' Kim's own voice sounded alien to her, husky. Hearing it made her finally aware that she wasn't dreaming. One of the figures turned and walked towards her. There was something odd about her, tall and hipless beneath her overall, long black hair piled on her head. She stood by the bed.

'Frankly, no.' Kim started at hearing the gutteral, London tones and at seeing the stubble on his chin. She rolled over onto her back and opened her mouth to shout, but the man was there first, a rough hand

clenched over her jaws, pursing and pinching her lips
in its palm, squeezing her cheeks together painfully
with wrist and fingers. Her attempt at noise came out
as a series of long, muffled 'o's, and for a second she
beat her fists on the bed in pain. Silly move –
he took the moment to vault onto the bed and, sitting
himself astride her like a cowboy mounting a moving
horse, he pinioned her arms to her sides with his legs,
his knees digging painfully into her tits, braless
beneath the flimsy satin. Her ribs already felt bruised.

He raised his other hand. Kim's eyes widened as
she saw that it held a thick roll of tape, the thickness
of duct tape but curiously shiny – pervy black and
shiny. He placed one end as carefully as he could over
her mouth, gripping it between the thumb and
forefinger of the hand that still gagged her, and
wound the reel brutally around the back of her head
until the tape dug painfully into the base of her skull
and it returned to overlap the tape already on her
mouth. Inching his gagging hand aside, he wound the
tape again and again around Kim's jaw with increasing speed. When he was sure that there was enough
to prevent her opening her jaw and dislodging it, he
pulled her head forwards with a sharp tug of her hair,
the faster to wind the remainder and seal her mouth
closed for sure.

Kim squirmed, her cries reduced to muffled yelps.
She could smell the industrial smell of the tape
beneath her nostrils. Her cheeks pulled painfully
against it as she tried to move her jaw. She could do
nothing. If only he weren't straddling both her arms.
She tried to tug them upwards but they wouldn't
budge. Beneath his thighs, her hands scrabbled furiously for some way to express her rage and panic –
to *do* something, clawing at the rough denim of the
jeans he wore underneath the overall. All of a sudden

she felt his scrotum beneath her fingertips, drawn up, compacted against the base of his penis as though the rest of it were erect, although, feeling from behind, Kim couldn't be sure. Bending her fingers around until her wrists cramped, she was able to take his balls between her thumbs and forefingers. With both hands, she gave an almighty squeeze. She watched his grizzled features grimace as he moaned and made an effort to raise himself away from her. Kim released his balls, taking the chance to draw her arms up through his legs. He fell to one side of her on the bed. She reached a hand to his head, set to grab a handful of hair and dash him somewhere, anywhere, away from her, thinking too quickly to consider the wig, which came off in her hand.

From the foot of the bed, the other figure loomed, revealed now his partner had moved. This one was Japanese-looking, titless beneath the same nylon overall as his partner, but otherwise a more convincing woman, fine-featured beneath a second black wig. He was too far away for Kim's flailing, lashing arms to reach, and his face leered his advantage as he bent down calmly and grabbed Kim's ankle with both hands, gripping it like he was about to loosen a lid on a jar. Above the tight gag, Kim's eyes widened.

He twisted Kim's ankle firmly and fast so that, in one fluid move, she was forced to roll over on to her stomach. Her other leg thrashed blindly at him, her foot making contact somewhere, but it didn't seem to worry him. Unlike his partner, still moaning beside her, he seemed inured to pain. She supported herself on her hands for a second, as if ready for a wheelbarrow race, before her elbows gave out and she collapsed on to the fetid sheets.

His partner rolled away from her and on to his feet and, crouching slightly, made his way to the trolley.

He returned with some pre-cut lengths of red nylon rope, already looped into slipknots and, as the Japanese guy pinned her ankles to the bed, ensuring she couldn't kick and that she stayed on her stomach, sat beside her. His black hair was beetle-like, slicked back for the wig, obviously, incongruous above the nylon overall. She threw an arm at him, lashing out half-heartedly, spent from her futile struggle, and he grabbed her wrist easily. There was no sound in the room now but the rustle of Kim's satin pyjamas and her muffled squeal as he twisted her arm hard, bending it around and curling it up her back until her shoulder ached and she heard the seam of her sleeve tear a little in her armpit. Her wrist was behind her neck, her face pushed further into the bed, and she twisted her head to make sure she could still draw air through her nostrils. Their eyes met and he leered broadly, recovered now. Hers flashed panic and hate.

With that, he swung himself across her a second time. Taking her other arm, he wrenched it up painfully to join the first, pinioning her wrists together behind her neck in his large grip. Putting his full weight on her, his bony ass in the small of her back, pressing her abdomen painfully against the sheets, he squeezed his knees to bring her elbows together between them, forcing her shoulder blades out like chicken wings, forearms flush together between them, muscles aching like she'd worked out without warming up.

With his free hand, he slipped a coil of the rope down her wrists to her elbows, where he pulled the slipknot tight. Then he wound the scratchy nylon rope around the outside of her elbows too, pulling them even closer together and ensuring that the rope would not slip up towards her wrists. With a practised hand, he looped the end around the sections of rope which sat in the space between her elbows, straining like hawsers against the natural outward pull of her aching arm muscles, cutting into her flesh through the creased satin although she had been bound in wide bands, doubtless already patterning her skin.

His partner, meanwhile, had gone to work on her legs. He had slipped a length of rope around her knees, looped over itself in between them, and passing down to her ankles which he was now fastening together just as surely despite her wriggling feet. Next Kim felt the rough rope pulled hard around her wrists, and she began to sob into the gag. Her thoughts had gone haywire; what the hell was this? She felt hot tears roll across the bridge of her nose, on to her pillow. She could hear only their breathing now, betraying not excitement so much as methodical concentration, like workers in a meat-packing plant, as they worked seamlessly to truss her. With the fastening of her wrists, her bondage seemed complete, but still the man on her back found rope enough to loop the end first around one arm just beneath the shoulder, and then around the other, between her arms and her torso. He pulled this tight and tied it off, checking it was securely fastened with a firm tug which lifted Kim from the bed for a second, pulling her arms back further and causing her tits to jut out beneath her, before she was dropped back on to the mattress.

The man above her dismounted and the man at her feet must have stepped away. Their handiwork was complete for now. Kim forced her muscles against her bonds, straining and pushing in all directions and kicking out wildly with her bound feet as one. But the only movement possible was to shuck herself up and down on the mattress in a parody of sexual rutting, arching her waist up and, finding purchase with her feet, pushing it down again. This had the effect only of moving her a little towards the head of the bed, like some bizarre omniped. Shit – out of sight, they were laughing at her, chuckling and sniggering in low masculine tones. She stopped, defeated, and relaxed into her bonds dejectedly as awareness of her helplessness descended on her thoughts like a shroud.

Then the Japanese man took her by the ankles once more – both this time – and twisted her on to her right side, facing the man whose balls she had twisted. She was glad she had got that in now. Her breasts fell slightly towards the bed under the thin satin, their undersides slipping against her chest with the sheen of sweat she had worked up. She saw him glance at them, and at her hip, where, wordlessly, he placed a hand. He ran it down her sheathed legs and back up again, over the arc of her hips to her waist, curiously gentle, affectionate. Barely touching her skin at times, his fingertips felt like feathers, in contrast to her painfully tight bonds. But at the same time their very presence against her was a warning. Her body had ached anew from each fresh twist, shafts of pain crisscrossed her nervous system. She lay fearful, expectant, and drew up her bound knees foetally.

He continued to brush his fingers against her, contemplating her as she lay, silent beneath her gag, watching him. He was only in his mid-twenties, she guessed, young to be so self-assured, and she took in his face properly for the first time: hooded eyelids with soft black lashes, chin stubble, the dents of multiple piercings visible but empty; stripped down for attack; leaving nothing that could be ripped out should his prisoner prove recalcitrant, she guessed.

And then he spoke quietly, in his low tones a measured threat. 'You shouldn't have done that . . .' With his other hand he gestured to his groin, almost coyly, like an old friend she'd wronged, like he had a place to be hurt about it. 'I was only playing. See? This tape is bondage tape . . .' He picked up the roll from where he'd left it on the bedside table and brought it to eye-level, shiny and smelly-new. 'It's sticks only to itself. Expensive too. I could have just bought duct tape, fucked up your hair and everything. You think a leg-waxing's bad – try getting that stuff off.' He spoke like a tradesman justifying his workmanship, insisting he'd sourced all the best parts. Kim almost felt sorry.

She felt him pause in his caress. Then, without warning, he brought his flat palm down fast and hard on to her ass, globed since she had drawn up her knees, the satin sheer against it, and her mind was rent by pain and alarm. She breathed hard through flaring nostrils, eyes wild with an affrontedness which made her cough and splutter into the gag. He took her by the chin, tender once more, and raised her face to his. Full of empathy, ignoring her anger, like someone else had hurt her and he had just happened along, he spoke softly once more, as her bound shoulders shook, her body racked with anguish beneath its smooth sheen, 'You're not about to choke, are you?' Foolishly, she looked at him and shook her head. Damn! Of course she hadn't been thinking, but she'd missed a chance to have her mouth free to breathe, free to shout. She cursed herself. He'd tricked her into being honest with his friendly tone. She understood why kidnap victims sometimes spoke of a bond with their captors; when someone shows concern for you in such a barren landscape, the kindness is amplified, even if they've created the environment in the first place.

'There, now we're quits,' he added as Kim lay prostrate, afraid even to wriggle, silent now as he stroked her hair gently, running a thumb under her eyes to trace her freckles and wipe away her tears. So confused was she that even had she not been bound she might have let him, grateful for anyone's comfort right then. But if he had the notion that they'd be in any way 'quits' unless she'd dragged him through the courts, he must be delusional. How come he acted like he had some right to be here, doing this?

Then a penny dropped and a realization dawned, an option she'd been hitherto too panicked, straight from sleep, to consider, and the image formed of Andy, her boyfriend, on the phone, back in California, under the friendly skies she was missing now, explaining his plans for surprising a lady he knew who was kinky as hell and had a few days spare in London. Did these guys seem like the unseen takers of the call in her imagination? They were the kind of guys, she now guessed, that Andy might know; the kind who could tell the difference between bondage tape and duct tape. If she was wrong about them being from Andy then she should be even more terrified, but even supposing they were, could she afford to feel secure? He'd so far repaid her trust, sure, but she wasn't sure if she could trust his judgement of character when it came to getting others to play complex games. She'd never had to before. But for now, trussed like a package, abused as she was, it was her best hope.

The second man joined his partner at the side of the bed and spoke to him in equally broad London tones, drawing his rapt gaze from Kim. 'Don't you think we ought to take the laundry out now?'

'Yeah, you're right,' he said reluctantly. Standing to face Kim, he raised a foot to her, its Doc Marten boot incongruous with the flimsy overall covering his street clothes. Placing it on her hip, he pushed her on to her back, leaving a dirty boot print on the satin. There was a sharp pain in her arms, concertinaed as they were, folded in on themselves like a music stand and now supporting the weight of her torso. Her tits stood proudly with no help from her, her chest forced out, her sore abdominal muscles straining as she straightened her legs.

Curiously, they left her there and returned to the trolley, lifting off the topmost metal tray and placing it carefully, full of cleaning materials and – she now realised – red ropes, on the floor. This left a single, stronger tray at the base, a metal strut at each corner, on which they spread out what looked like a large, webbed sack. As they unfurled it, Kim noticed the word 'laundry' stencilled on the side. They worked quickly to lift her off the bed, helpless as she was to help herself, and place her on her feet in the middle of the trolley. She cast a glance ruefully at the phone by the bed; the last conduit of help whose receiver her hands were not free to lift, its message light blinking in vain. Trapped, they wriggled almost comically behind her head. Taking an arm each and supporting her on either side, they let her slide into a kneeling position beneath them as her wobbly legs gave way. They had no reason to be other than gentle; this was obviously how they'd wanted her anyway.

The Japanese-looking man dropped to one knee beside her and spoke softly, measuredly, in her ear. 'Now, Kim, we like you, so far . . .' Kim gasped – as much as she could behind the tape – and he paused as she raised her wide eyes to his, thoughts tumbling through her mind: they knew who she was. So they were not random attackers out to use just anyone. She was not an heiress, no ransom potential, no rich relatives. Their presence *must* be Andy's doing . . . But she had to snap back into listening mode as he

177

began to talk once more, '. . . so being the gents we are, we'll give you the chance to co-operate with us, which we can make you do anyway, so if you sit tight, keep quiet, things will be a little easier than they might be otherwise.' To reinforce his point, he gave her shoulder a little shove.

With that, the other guy came into view. He had replaced his wig, but there was another surprise: slung across his oustretched arms was a leather yoke, a broad black strip about a foot long, covered with soft purple fur, real too, on one side. Chains hung from eyelets at each end. In one hand he held a padlock. He placed the yoke behind her head, between the soft satin and her bound wrists, her bunched hands, and let the chains fall either side of her neck, brushing her nipples as their pendulum motion came to rest, their ends swinging just above her knees, only an inch or two from the trolley base. The fur was warm, comforting through the satin at the nape of her neck. She felt drained. There was no point in struggling.

The Japanese man pushed her firmly forwards from behind, the flat of a palm on her poor sore elbows, then the sole of a boot, until she was compacted into an S-shape while he stood above her. Her tits were squashed against her knees and she felt the chains being drawn taut at her cleavage; the man whose balls she had twisted had passed behind her and now he snicked the padlock through the chain links, fastening them together around the knot between her ankles, and suddenly she could raise her body no higher. She wondered just how much of a grudge he bore. She had been trussed and tied until she could flex no limbs whatsoever. When she tried, twisting her limbs, pushing up uselessly with her back and legs, growling into her gag in frustration, she succeeded in moving her head up and down a little, but that was it. She heard the men behind her chuckle at her attempts, and it occurred to her how her little ass must look; twin globes beneath taut satin, prone and defenceless, framing a hole protected only by the elastic of her waistband, one cheek still smarting, a reminder that she was under another's discipline now.

They were talking *about* her not to her, like she was a gallery exhibit, as they busied themselves with the sides of the sack, its large drawstring circling her like a chalk mark at some bizarre ritual of which she was the focus. Bunching it in their palms, they began to pull it up around her prone form and, though completely black, she could see that it was made of a breathable, tentlike nylon material which rustled as they pulled it around her.

'Wait a minute,' said the western man, 'I'll forget where I put this if I don't leave it somewhere obvious.' And he drew from his pocket a padlock key tied to a long red loop of ribbon. Helplessly Kim's eyes followed his hands as he placed it around her neck, almost reverentially, like he were conferring a chain of office, and one hand passed inside her pyjamas as he pushed it securely into her cleavage alongside the chains, brushing the top of each breast with his cold knuckles, making them wobble as much as they could in their squashed state. It occurred to Kim that this was the closest either of them had come to touching her sex organs – the spank being a moot point – and yet she had anticipated it all along, and she wondered only now if there'd been any degree of alacrity in that anticipation. 'After all,' he continued, turning to Kim this time, 'you wouldn't want to be stuck like this, would you?' It entered her head to reply as best she could, and she shook her head and mewed at him as the nylon bag continued its rise around her.

Eventually, sightless now in dark, fusty air, she heard the drawstring pulled tight by the would-be chambermaids. She imagined herself marked 'do not disturb'. Next she felt the upper tray pressed hard against her arms, squashing them into her back still further. The surface above her meant that she no longer had room to nod her head. Short of muffled whines, she was now deprived of any way to alert anyone to her presence. She looked like nothing other than a bag of dirty washing.

As the trolley moved, it seemed to shake new pain from her poor tortured joints, teasing out each ache further all the time, relentlessly. Her feet, stretched out behind her, were beginning to cramp, her knees were already getting sore against the hard metal. She heard the door to her room clunk closed behind them. They were into the corridor and wheeling her fast, their passage punctuated by the rhythmic squeaking of one wheel. It was the noise, she realised, that had woken her, repeated now to taunt her again and again, and drown out any squeaking of her own. She was being wheeled inexorably towards her fate, whatever it was, like a prisoner led to execution, forced to prostrate herself as if in supplication.

What would they do, she wondered. Leave her trussed and abandoned somewhere? And what if those who chanced upon her took their cue from how they'd found her? Feeding and cleaning, maintaining her for their pleasure. Perhaps all the men who chanced upon her would treat her thus, popping back when they needed to . . . relieve themselves, and she'd remain there by a silent conspiracy, talked of in dark corner bars, the Neighbourhood Slut.

5

Submission

Bitchboys, pain and imperious Mistresses

- Nothing in this book crystallises the difference between fantasy and reality better perhaps than the numerous respondents who fantasise about not being able to come, presumably while doing just that!
- And nothing demonstrates more than the penultimate reply in this chapter that submissive sexuality can, as likely as not, be associated with the powerful psychological impression and explosive associations left by past injustice to the self. Of all of the fantasies in this book, no other made me more conscious that I was dealing with the real feelings of real people. If the Stockholm Effect is the phenomenon by which kidnap victims come to regard their captors with love or at least benign warmth, then one might label the same thing as applied to corporal punishment the 'Eton Effect'. Personally, I deplore violence against children and look forward to the day when smacking, even, let alone old-school CP as practised back in the day, is clearly illegal.

- There's a wider point here: about CP as an indicator of a CP fan's social politics, as against those whose interest lies in the sexual and sensual appeal alone. If it's disappointing to encounter those who literal-mindedly associate kinky fun with sexual violence, it's equally if not more disappointing to meet a CP enthusiast who, it turns out, actually thinks judicial birching as practised in Singapore or Rhiyad is a Good Thing.
- Nexus does not condone the non-consensual administration of drugs as a means of seduction.

Another: aged 20-plus in the 50s. I imagine myself to have just graduated, and to have called on an older rich relation, a doctor who is partly crippled, to get summer employment. After some chat, since it is very hot he tells me to go down the big garden and have a swim in the big pool there, making me feel faintly prudish when he brushes aside my objection that I have no swimming costume with me, I will find towels. I have never swum naked before, after fifteen minutes he appears in his wheel-chair pushed by his grey-uniformed and very pretty employee, orders me to come out and be examined if I want a job, when I object he says that the girl is a nurse and will take no notice. I am (in my imagination), as he comments, a very strong and well-set-up young fellow, and he – I nearly control my embarrassment – holds my testicles to test for ruptures. 'What do you think?' he says to her. 'I want to see it up,' she answers, and takes her slightly uneven breasts out of her dress. Though I am not a virgin my sexual experiences have been in dark corners and though I have felt breasts I have never seen them, I am immediately erect. She approves. I am employed that summer because my uncle can no longer have intercourse or masturbate much, to have intercourse or to be masturbated either by him or by her or both to amuse them. Now I am old and imagine myself rich I wonder whether to employ a young couple for much the same purposes, decide against it, I remember that summer not as being in any way degrading, but restrictive, never believing myself free.

* * *

I am replying to your ad in *Desire* concerning the fantasies of men.

I have always been an avid wanker. Started off with mags, videos – Fiona Cooper type not hardcore. Occasionally look at hardcore porn, particularly if it has a scene with a posh woman in it who looks dominant. I tend to associate dom women with vigorous sex.

I enjoy frottage and like to rub against a woman's body till I come.

Prefer having sex with one woman at a time but like other women to watch me have sex. Enjoy wanking in front of a group of women. Enjoy chatting on the phone while wanking. Love to be teased and tortured by dominant women.

Find lots of women attractive for different reasons: could be their figure, personality or eagerness to please.

Went through phase of sniffing items of clothing. Usually knickers, sometimes shoes.

Sometimes wank into a pair of knickers or rub cock against fur to climax.

Ultimate fantasy for me would be to find a woman who was the following: dominant; sexy prick-teaser; talks to me and gives me a wet dream; high sex drive; voyeur; likes to be wanked off; exhibitionist – stripper or prostitute; enjoys prolonged penetration of cunt;

enjoys role-play – wearing uniforms/glasses; experienced enough to make me come twice; probably a prostitute.

I do enjoy the prim secretary scenario, who is really a dirty whore who needs a good fucking. Slim with glasses and a rude temper, and very efficient. I would like to watch a woman in an office do a striptease and turn me on.

The sound of a woman's shoes can sometimes be a turn-on, especially when I'm frustrated and need a fuck.

Women's tits can give me a hard-on or make my balls rise. As can bums or legs. Upskirt photos/mags usually produce hard-on if picture or face is familiar. I am not the only man that enjoys drooling over a woman walking along, thinking of what sex they could have and where. And then wakes up to reality but usually fantasises about the woman later on.

Will close now. Hope some of this may be of use to you.

*　*　*

This is a letter I wrote to my girlfriend when she asked me to write down some of my (many) fantasies. I hope this is the kind of thing you are looking for.

As a submissive, most of my fantasies revolve around dominant (and usually slightly older) women with a taste for various leather, PVC and latex clothes. It's my aim to try and write as many of my fantasies down as I can bring to mind.

The Boss: She is my boss at work, she's older, experienced and dressed in a skirt-suit, her hair is black, tied up and immaculate. I have been asked to work late in the office, she has also stayed back and spends much of the time carelessly flirting with me. She sits on my desk and drinks coffee, chatting while I work, her legs crossed exposing the lacy tops of her stockings. I continue to work knowing that she knows I have seen what she is wearing. A short while passes and she calls me in her office. She asks me if I like working for her and how far I want to take my career. I stand nervously as she walks around her desk and sits on it crossing her legs as before . . . she unbuttons her jacket exposing a crisp white shirt, her breasts are pulling the buttons apart and the aroma of her heady perfume and coffee mixes as she chats to me. She asks me to take a seat on her leather chesterfield and offers me a drink from her cabinet. I have a vodka and as she pours it (large) she pulls the pins out of her hair and lets it hang down her back. She sits next to me on the sofa and again crosses her leg, she chats about me, my wife/girlfriend, her husband and work but carefully places her hand on my lap. She can see the bulge in my trousers and loosens my tie for me. She sits back on her sofa and opens her legs exposing herself. Gesturing towards her pussy she makes it quite clear that I could go far in her company, kind of a 'you scratch my back . . . I'll scratch yours' situation. I end up on my knees pleasuring her in the quiet of her office as she uses my tie to pull herself on to me, never getting to fuck her . . . only ever oral. Needless to say this happens often and my career is safe.

Bi women: I'm in a club, standing on my own just having a break from it all while my friends chat. I notice a woman looking at me, she is wearing a pair of strappy sandals, a knee-length leather pencil skirt and a tailored leather top which has long sleeves and is slightly unzipped exposing her cleavage . . . Her nails are long and dark as is her lipstick and eye make-up. She only looks, smiles, looks me up and down and seductively drinks her wine as we stare at each other across the club, just then a friend of hers returns, She hands her a drink and I watch as they whisper to each other. Her friend is shorter and has long blonde hair, she looks up at her friend who has only just looked away from me and they kiss, I can't believe it as I watch, I feel a little disappointed but horny at the same time and I look away. I stand with my back to them and watch my friends chatting as I relive what I just saw over and over in my mind. I never turn back but I don't need to . . . her friend comes over and stands in front of me and asks me if I'd like to have a drink with them. I'm a little shocked but I don't need asking twice. I stand with them and the tall leather-clad one asks me if I'd like to go to a little club with them. I look at my friends who have seen where I am and decided to move on, I agree and we go to the club. While in the club we dance, never really talking and they both begin to flirt with me, rubbing up against me. One of them feels my trousers and suggests we share a taxi home. It's a London cab-style taxi and we all sit in the back, the girls on the seat and me with my back to the driver. They tell the driver where to go and he begins driving, as we drive the girls begin kissing each other obviously trying to make me horny . . . it works. The cab pulls up outside their flat and the tall one gets out first, her leather skirt squeaking as she climbs past me, then her friend. They pay the driver while I sit in the back and they look at me and say 'you coming?' I get out of the cab and they take me inside! They offer me a drink and I sit in the middle of their sofa, they sit either side of me and begin to seduce me . . . quite roughly.

A slave: I imagine myself being stripped of my individuality, having my entire personality erased and being the plaything of three dominant women (sometimes it's just one woman), kept hooded, booted and cuffed, having no 'normal' clothes, never being allowed out unless accompanied. All my personal belongings gone and having nothing but the items I am wearing to my name. Never needing money or possessions. Contact with my former life ended so that my whole world is my life contract to these women. My body made in the image of the Dominant, pierced, marked and tattooed wherever they choose. Forced to change my physique in ways to please them. Being used (but loved) as they please and being punished when they choose.

Feeling cheap: I receive a letter in the post. It has a time and the name of a bar (next to a hotel) with instructions. The instructions are simple . . . a short list of things to bring. I arrive in the bar and it's early, a woman is sitting on a bar stool, her short black leather skirt has risen slightly exposing her stocking tops on her crossed legs. The creases in her white shirt are perfect, her long painted nails extend from her finger tips as she seductively holds a lit cigarette which has her dark lipstick on the butt. Through her shirt I can see a black bra and a tattoo on her shoulder. I look as she picks up her empty wine glass and swills it as if to say 'I'm thirsty' so I walk over and buy her a drink, she asks me if I have brought everything she asked for and drinks her wine. She puts her cigarette out and stands up. I help her on with her short leather biker jacket and she pulls her gloves on. She leads me across the road to the hotel pausing to let me pick my bag up. She has booked herself in to the hotel and she walks me to the lift. It opens and is empty, it travels slowly to the top floor and she comes close to me, the smell of alcohol, smoke, leather and perfume drives me wild. In the room she takes off only her jacket leaving the leather gloves on, she sits on an armchair next to the table which has a selection of drinks on it. She crosses her legs and tells me to get changed then pour her a drink. I head for the bathroom but she insists I stay and undress in front of her. I put on what I was asked to bring and pour her drink, she takes out another cigarette and holds it between her gloved fingers, tosses me the lighter and I light it. She holds it up and blows smoke at me. She knows I don't like it but she does not care . . . She makes me sit at her feet and has me do things like pleasure her, play with myself for her amusement, forces me to drink till I'm drunk, lick her shoes clean, bathe her and massage her body. She drips neat vodka in my mouth from the tip of her riding crop and makes me bend over so she can spank me (and other things). This continues all night until late then she has me put on my PVC catuit and hood and makes me sleep at her feet. When I wake in the morning she has gone but she has left a note saying the room has been paid for and a brand new, crisp twenty-pound note for my services which makes me feel used and cheap. I put the money in my wallet and leave quietly having not been allowed to relieve myself all night.

Forceful women: I am visiting someone, a woman I consider to be a good friend, she is slightly older than me and very attractive. We have had a coffee together in town and she has asked me for a lift home as her car is in for repair. We drive back to her place and she asks if I'd like another drink, I agree and we go up to her flat. We chat aimlessly about things and she mentions that there is something wrong with her bedside clock (or something else in the bedroom) and asks if I could take a look for her. We have a coffee and she shows me where the bedroom is, I begin looking at the clock and start to try and fix it. She begins to go through her wardrobe and takes out a few items of clothing and tells me she has a date and wants my opinion on what to wear ... she shows me a knee-length leather pencil skirt and a shorter leather miniskirt. Feeling horny I suggest she wears the long one as it will make her look slender and she suggests that she tries it on. I watch as she turns her back to me and unzips her trousers, they fall to her ankles revealing a pair of sexy hold-up fishnets and no knickers. I am transfixed until I realise she is watching me watch her in her mirror so I blush and turn away. I continue to look at the clock and she walks over to me, I'm sitting on the edge of the bed and she tells me that she thinks I'm right and that the long one feels so much better. She sits next to me as I fumble with the clock and she begins to say things about how this side of the bed was her husband's and she gets lonely from time to time, she tells me that it's not just men who have their needs. As I finish sorting the clock out, I feel her hand on my thigh and I tell her I'm all done, she pushes me back on her bed and tells me I have only just started. I try to sit up, pushing against her but not using a fraction of my strength and she pushes me back down. She tells me to stop fighting it, it's only sex, mutual pleasure and if I don't, she'll tell my girlfriend that I have been sleeping with her. She is rubbing my crotch through my jeans and I'm getting harder. I still resist but she pushes herself next to me. She tells me that she knows I want it and shouldn't deprive myself. I want to touch her skirt but don't because she'll know I want her too and that will mean she has won. Again I try to get up and this time she slides her skirt up and sits across me, the tops of her fishnets are exposed again and I slowly move my hand towards her ass where the leather of her skirt is pulled tight. She grabs my hands and holds them to the bed and comes in close telling me to just fuck her. I tell her I can't and she argues that if I don't, my girlfriend will think I have . . . if I do . . . she'll never know. She begins to rub her pussy against me and I ask her to stop as she'll mark my jeans and she tells me I had better take them off then. I refuse and she whispers in my ear again . . . telling me to fuck her, make her come. She reaches between my leg and feels that I'm hard, and unzips my jeans . . . as she forces herself on to my cock I still act as though I'm refusing her but I want it now . . . my gasps of, *'No, please stop,'* slowly become *'Yes, fuck me,'* occasionally feeling a little guilt only to be met by more force and aggression from the woman.

Drugs: I imagine myself having a drink or something to eat with a very horny and dominant woman. She has prepared the food/drink especially for me and we eat together . . . I slowly begin to feel different, very different. My body is tingling and I begin to feel spaced out . . . I ask what I had just eaten and she casually mentions that she has drugged me with something. I try to get up but I'm uneasy on my feet so she helps me and suggests I lie down and she'll get me something to take that will make me better. I lay on her bed and she gives me a tablet, by now I'm so spaced out everything seems different, my senses are heightened and I'm totally buzzing all over. She returns with a glass of water and I take the tablet and drink the water . . . she begins to undress me and I feel my cock getting hard, as she undresses herself she asks me if I had ever taken *Viagra* before, I hear what she has said but it does not register in my head . . . I feel 'out of myself' and she slides herself on to my drug-induced erection and begins to pleasure herself being very loud and horny as she does. The Viagra works well and the drugs do not wear off for quite some time. Long enough for me to feel spaced out and for her to pleasure herself on me several times.

I do have a return address but I'd appreciate it if you didn't address me as 'Bitchboy'. I'd also appreciate it if you didn't use my real name wherever you use them! Thanks!

Bitchboy 2002

* * *

Dear Sir

I have read your advert in *Desire Direct* and though not being too sure of exactly what you are looking to attract I would like to express an interest. I have attached an article which I prepared a short time ago which is in the main a true reflection of one incident in my school life.

I am a middle-aged man who attended a boys-only grammar school during that period when CP was actively practised in the schools. I therefore received during my five years at that school a number of spankings and canings. Up to the end of my school life I hated this and dreaded being sent to the head for the cane.

However within a short time of leaving school I fantasised about being back there and being in the head's study, totally naked, receiving the cane on my backside. I married and for 22 years did receive regular 'punishment' as part of our love/role play. I am now divorced which makes my search for punishment that bit more difficult and I have to settle for interest on the internet and through magazines such as *Desire*.

All of my accounts of what happenned to me re. CP at school I have written up and I have also written about my punishment sessions into 'adulthood'. This writing has gone one stage further in that I have also written about fantasy CP but each of these stories features girls being punished rather than me.

If you want me to send you samples of these writings I will do so. My personal background is that I am five foot nine inches tall slim-ish and have a full-time professional job. No day passes however without me thinking about CP.

If I have got your advert totally wrong then please 'bin' the sample I have sent you!

Caned at School Aged 16 with my Mother as Witness

This is a true story of the last caning I received at school aged 16 years. I had been in trouble before at this boys-only grammar school and had been caned on five previous occasions by the head but this one was by far the most painful and most embarrassing. At the time of this caning I hated it and it was one of the reasons why I left school the following summer. But reflecting on it now I find it very erotic and I love wherever I can to be back in that situation.

Back to the occasion at school. I did not 'skive' off school like many of my friends did but on this one occasion I did when I was offered a cheap deal on a minibus to travel one hundred miles away to watch my football team play an evening league game.

Not to this day have I any idea as to how the school found out I was playing truant but find out they did. Whilst I was away watching my team lose 3–0 my mum and the head's secretary were planning a suitable punishment for me.

When I arrived home after eleven p.m. my mother asked how my time at a mate's house had gone. I said yes it went well we did loads of homework. My mum then said was it homework about football and at this point I realised I was going to be in trouble. I decided to admit the truth and tried to convince my mum that I did not miss anything vital at school but she was having none of this. She said that she had had a long telephone conversation with the head's secretary late that afternoon about the actions the head wanted to take against me. My heart started to jump at this point when my mum said it was either expulsion and a report to the local authority or it was 'six of the best' with the cane. My mum told me that they had both decided that it was too crucial a time to lose schooling and so they had decided on the caning. The situation got worse when my mum added that they had agreed that I should receive the cane on my bottom dressed only in PE shorts and that my mother would witness the event. I was told that I had to come out of class just before 11 a.m. the next day then go to the gym area and to change into my PE shorts. I was then to walk over to the head's study where I would meet my mother and wait outside the door until the head called us in. I would then be caned very hard across my bottom six times and my mother would watch.

As I didn't have many negotiating rights I spent a very restless night and didn't want any breakfast the following morning. As I left the house for school my mother said 'see you at 11 o'clock' and have I got with me my PE shorts. I had tried to deliberately forget them but my mum said that would be OK – if I didn't have the shorts I would receive the caning on my bare backside. I hurriedly returned to my bedroom for the shorts.

I wasn't able to concentrate on lessons during the first part of the morning and that got me into trouble with the geography teacher. Towards the end of the lesson, having had to warn me to concentrate three times before, he ordered me out to the front of the class. He asked me if anything was troubling me and I said no and he said that he would give me a reminder about what he expected in his lessons from us boys. At that point when he went to his front desk and brought out his favourite raggie slipper I knew the drill. Without being asked I bent over his front desk until my chin was touching the desk ready for my spanking. He asked me how many slaps I should be given and I said one. He said try again and I said two. He said try again and I said three and he said good. For the next minute or so I was given three hard slaps with that slipper with every other boy in the class watching. Somehow this didn't appear important with respect of what was about to happen to me in the head's study.

After the end of the geography lesson I went to the toilet and tried to be sick. I then went to the gym changing rooms and changed into my PE shorts. I then started the slow embarrassing walk to the head's study. This took me across many parts of the school and I got some funny looks from boys who were wondering what I was doing. Some other boys worked out what was to happen to me and I got comments such as 'those canings do hurt don't they – particularly when the only protection is a thin pair of shorts'. I ignored all these comments but I knew that most of them were accurate.

I eventually reached the head's area of the school. My mum was already sat waiting for me and said I was two minutes late and why was I delayed? I simply said I couldn't get away from my last lesson. My mum said that if the head asked to give you extra strokes for lateness she would back this. By this time all my resistance had gone anyway and I didn't react to this. The secretary who had played a big part in me being here this day ushered us in to the head's room. I immediately noticed that he had on his big desk a vicious-looking cane.

With a very stern face he looked at me then changed his expression when greeting my mum. He shook hands with her and said that it would have been better to have met in a more favourable way though he was pleased that she had supported the school. He then turned his attentions back to me and said that according to school records I had been in this office five times before and each time had been given the cane. I said nothing but my mum exclaimed surprise. Wherever I could avoid it I didn't tell my parents about the canings that I had received before. The head went on that I would know what to do and I nodded yes. He then said move into the centre of the room and assume the position. I slowly went to the middle of the room; looked at the head for his approval; he nodded back and I bent over and touched my toes whilst keeping my legs straight and with my feet about twelve inches apart. He suggested to my mum that she should move behind me so that she could get a good view of the caning that was to follow. She did this and the head brought her a chair. He moved behind me and said the offence I had committed was one of the most serious and often led to expulsion. In this case though since my mum and dad had expressed it, this would be changed into a 'six of the best' caning. He went on to say that this caning would be much harder than any I had received before, and I was to brace myself for this. I said nothing. The head said that the same rules apply. If

I move during the session then the caning would start again. I was also required to thank the head for each stroke and to count the number. I nodded that I understood. I noticed out of the corner of my eye that the head had raised the cane high above himself and I closed my eyes and held my breath. I then heard a whoosh noise followed by a crack and with instant severe pain in my buttocks more to the right side than the left. Even though I was in great pain I said 'one headmaster, thank you for caning me'. The head turned to my mum and asked if what he had done was OK for her and she said yes carry on he does deserve the most severe caning.

For the next few minutes I received the most severe of canings that I had had to take. How I didn't move or cry out is still beyond me and how I managed to thank him and count the number is something I am still proud of. After stroke six he told me to stay where I was and he, plus my mum came up to me from behind. The head moved my shorts down slightly until he could see where the cane had landed and both said what a good sight it was. My mum said I should receive extra strokes for being late and the head said he would leave that to whatever the parents decided later at home. I did not understand the significance of this until later that evening.

I was then told I could stand up and was to put my hands on my head and to go and stand in the corner. This I did although walking was painful. My mum and the head then had a cup of tea each and made the entry in the school punishment book. Five minutes later I was told I could go and change and return to class.

I then went painfully back to class which was a physics session. The teacher asked me why I was late and I said I had had an appointment with the head.

Some of the boys laughed since they had worked out that I had been caned. The teacher said had I been disciplined and I said yes. He took pity on me and asked if I needed to go to the toilet but I said no. I sat down very painfully.

At the end of that day I went home as normal. My mum asked if I was OK and I snapped at her. She said it wasn't her fault that I had got into trouble and that her action had stopped me getting expelled. The state I was in didn't enable me to appreciate that.

About an hour later we had our evening meal. Dad had come home from work and my elder brother and his girlfriend were having a meal with us. My dad asked if I had taken the caning well and I said would he not raise it when we had guests. He said he would decide what was said in this house and repeated had I taken the caning well. I didn't answer but my mum said I had taken it very well. My dad said my mood could get me into trouble if I was not careful. My mum said she did want to discuss this but would wait until later. My dad, in an angry mood himself, said he wanted mum to explain now. She went on to say that I had arrived for my caning two minutes late and the head had said that we should sort that out in the home. My dad said why was I late but didn't like the answer that I gave. The room went silent whilst we ate the food.

After the meal my dad said that he didn't like my manner and that he felt it would be a good idea to knock some respect into me. I started to get nervous since I knew that this meant a slippering or a caning and I feared that it might be the latter. I started to grovel but too late – my dad said that I was to go upstairs to the landing cupboard and bring down the item from the inside of the door. I knew this was a hooked handle cane and said to dad please no more. He said I should have thought about this earlier.

My dad said he was going to give me six strokes of the cane to change my manner and if I didn't hurry up and fetch the cane he would double this. Within a few moments I had brought the cane downstairs and handed it to my dad. When I realised I wasn't going to avoid being caned again I started to ask if we could go to my bedroom so as to not embarrass our guest. My brother's girlfriend said she wasn't embarrassed and if she could be allowed to watch she would be grateful. She went on to say that she had often been caned by her dad and it was refreshing to watch someone else get it for a change. Refreshing was not the word I would have used.

My dad by now was practising his swing with the cane. He told me to move into the middle of the lounge. This I did and started to bend down. I was told to stand up and I wondered what was going on. He said he would cane me on my backside in a few minutes time but to start with I was to hold out my left hand. My dad hadn't hit me on my hands for sometime and the thought of it was not one I enjoyed. I held out my hand. My dad told me not to move it until I had received three strokes. My dad lifted the cane high into the air and brought it down with considerable force on to the palm of my hand. I squealed out loud since it really hurt me. I was told to shut up and the cane was raised again. It came down with even more force and it took all my resolve to not cry out. It was raised again and once more it crashed down on my hand causing me great pain. My dad said I could now take the hand down and rub it. Fifteen seconds later I was told to hold out my other hand. The treatment was repeated and again I suffered great pain. After stroke three my dad said I could now rub both hands. He said I could go to my room. I started to move and was told that in five minutes I had to come back down wearing only those PE shorts that I had had on for my school caning. I asked why I had to do this and my dad said that they had promised the school that I would receive a similar caning to the one earlier in the day. I started to protest to my dad that he couldn't do this to me with a guest in the house but my brother's girlfriend again said she was OK with this. My dad said that if I didn't hurry up and change he would cane me across my bare bottom. I hurried up! A few moments later I was back in the lounge wearing only those thin PE shorts which had taken such a battering earlier that day. My dad told me to move close to him in the centre of the room. He told me he was ashamed of me for playing truant and only the kindness of the head had stopped me from being expelled. I didn't agree that what I had received that day was being kind but I guess I was looking at the situation from a different painful angle?

My dad told me to place my hands on my head and I did as told. He told me I was to bend right over as far as I could manage. This position was a new one to me but since I knew what kind of mood my dad was in I did as I was told. So there I was bent right over with my bum presenting a clear target and with the rest of me totally naked and with my hands on my head. Any second now with my mum, my brother, my brother's girlfriend all watching I was going to be caned for the second time that day. I suspected that the caning I was about to receive might be as hard as the one earlier that day. Life seemed very unfair.

Without any warning my dad brought the cane down on to my bottom very hard. Since the marks from my first caning were still on my bum this first stroke hurt me more seriously than the first stroke of any previous caning. It may of course have had something to do with the fact that my dad had caned me very hard! I couldn't help myself and I jumped up and grabbed my bum and yelled out loud. My dad got very mad and told me to return to position and since I had moved that cane stroke wouldn't count. I glanced at my brother's girlfriend and detected that she had a smile on her face.

I reluctantly returned to the bent over position and for the next few minutes received a very heavy caning from my dad. After the seven strokes I started to stand up and my dad shouted at me again and told me he had not given permission to stand up. I quickly returned to the bent over position and prayed that my dad would not start my caning all over again. He must have decided that I had taken all the punishment I could for one day since he said I could now stand up.

He told me to face him and gave me one 'lecture' about my serious problem with behaviour and then said I could go to my room. I stayed in my room since I couldn't face going back to where this girlfried was and eventually composed myself. There was a knock on my door and though I didn't say 'enter' the door opened and my brother's girlfriend walked in. She sat on the edge of the bed and told me she thought I had taken the 'punishment' very well and that it had been a harder caning than she had ever had to take from her dad. She seemed to like talking in this way.

After a couple of minutes she returned downstairs to my brother. A strange thing then happened – reflecting on what had happened to me that day started to make me sexually excited! I will leave the rest to the reader's imagination. The significant issue here was although I had been caned and spanked many times before my only thoughts were how I hated the person punishing me. From this moment in my life all that changed.

I am now 52 and take opportunities whenever I can to be 'punished' and each time this happens I do get sexually aroused. Thus started my search for regular 'punishments' and these stories will be told later.

*   *   *

The Swinging Detective

My girlfriend Alison and I have found our sex life improving no end since we got into playing doctors and nurses. She has always taken the dominant role, but now she finds that when she plays the strict nurse and I am her helpless patient, she can push me to my very limits.

We have invested in a selection of equipment which we found via the fetish magazines and from some genuine medical suppliers, but the basic scene is always the same. I have been sent to the nurse for an intimate internal examination, and as I am somewhat apprehensive of what this will entail, the nurse has to take precautions to ensure that I do not attempt to leave or fight her off when she tries to examine me.

I am dressed in one of those white hospital patient's gowns which fastens at the neck and is loose all down the back of my body, to give her easy access to whichever part of me she wishes to inspect. Alison makes me lie face down on the couch – a rather unorthodox position for an internal examination, you might think – and then straps me firmly in place. The straps are made of wide leather and buckle in place, and offer me very little in the way of movement. However, I am able to move my head enough to watch Alison as she walks around the room, taking pieces of equipment from a low table.

She wears a breathtaking nurse's outfit, made from white rubber that clings to her gorgeous breasts and is so short it only just skims the curve of her ass. Sometimes, she will not wear any knickers beneath it, giving me tantalising flashes of her cunt, which I am not allowed to touch without her permission. My own cock and balls are kept shaven, and the first thing Nurse Alison does is inspect it to make sure I have not allowed any stubble to mar their wrinkledness. If I have, I know there will be trouble. This time, however, she is satisfied, and goes on to the next part of the examination.

She slips on a thin latex glove, and squeezes a generous dollop of lubricating jelly on to her rubber-clad fingers. As she bends over the table, I make the most of the brief glimpse the short uniform offers me of the contours of her beautiful pussy. She tells me she has to check that my anus is in good order, but warns me it may hurt a little. Erotically, she slips a first and then a second gloved, lubed finger into me, as if to see how widely I can stretch. On some occasions, she will use a speculum, knowing how much I hate the feel of the cold metal in my ass and pushing its walls apart but that I am powerless to prevent her. Her gloved fingers, now slippery with lubricating jelly, prise and manipulate the ring of muscle. I am growing increasingly excited, my arousal intensified by the impersonal way in which she is treating me, and I know that I will be in danger of coming without her permission. She acts as if she is completely oblivious to the state I am in as she disposes of the soiled latex glove in the swing-bin.

Time, she tells me, to examine my cock. Sometimes I use the pretence that I have made an appointment to visit her because I am worried about my inability to reach orgasm, and she wants to see exactly what is causing the problem. The point of this game is that I am to hold off from coming until she ascertains that everything is in complete working order and gives me her permission to do so, but by this time I am so turned on that it usually only takes the lightest few strokes of her fingers up and down my cock and I am spattering her clean uniform, bucking in orgasm, my movements restricted by the tight leather straps that bind me to the bed.

When this happens, Nurse Alison's demeanour changes abruptly as she tells me that such wanton behaviour in the clinical surroundings of the examination room is deserving of punishment. Usually, the form this punishment takes is that of an enema, which she thinks I hate. She unbuckles me from the couch to take me to the bathroom on my slightly shaky legs, where she has prepared a saline enema in advance. I am made to shed my hospital gown and crouch on all fours in the bath. The next thing I feel is the greased nozzle of the enema tube being inserted into my rectum and then the controlled flow of water flowing into my anal cavity. Nurse Alison loves to keep the water flowing until I am uncomfortably full and my whole abdomen is bobbling painfully with the need for relief. She likes me to beg her to stop, as she knows how humiliating I find the whole procedure. At last, she pulls out the tube and I want to scream with the joy of being able to void the water into the bath. The relief is so intense that I imagine I can feel my prostate tremble. If Nurse A is feeling kind, she will gently stroke my cock once more to messy completion. At last, I am allowed to shower, while Alison packs away all her equipment, ready for the next time she feels the need to give me such an intimate examination.

* * *

Greg and Anna were the first couple I got friendly with on the fetish scene. They took me under their wing when I turned up at my first ever club shaking in my leather trousers and not really sure what to expect. They introduced me to a lot of people, made me feel welcome and a part of the scene. They were also the only couple I knew who played where it wasn't easy to see who was the dominant and who the submissive as you can in most relationships. Sometimes Greg would be the master and Anna the sub and sometimes the roles would be reversed.

Before long, I had been fucked by both of them individually and together. When Anna was dominant she would wear a thick, black strap-on dildo protruding aggressively from her crotch, and she would order Greg or me to suck and she would thrust it hard and fast into Greg's lubed ass, till we were screaming with excitement. When Greg was in charge, he would order me to lick her pussy while she sucked my cock and he watched, then he would fuck either or both of us. So I would be feasting on Anna's juicy sex while sucking Greg's cock, and other times Anna's mouth would be nuzzling at my cock while Greg drove hard into me from behind. Until I met them I never realised I had the capacity to fuck or be fucked by a couple, but I had always known I wanted to be spanked and taken anally, and both of them were more than happy to indulge me in those fantasies.

I thought that a threesome would be the limits of my experience, but then Greg announced that a friend of his, Jon, was holding one of his special party evenings at his home in East London. I had heard about these parties, and knew that anything and everything could happen there, but attendance was strictly by invitation only, and that Jon and his wife, Maura, were very fussy about who joined their select circle. I was delighted and, I must admit, more than a little scared when Greg told me that Jon and Maura wanted me to be there, but that single men were invited only as slaves. Someone who was as willing to be used as I appeared to be would be very popular with the experienced masters and mistresses among Jon and Maura's group of friends.

The evening of the party, I spent a long time choosing what to wear. Greg had told me that, as a newcomer, I could expect to receive a lot of attention. Maura, in particular, liked to put new subs through their paces for the benefit of an audience, and though she could be very cruel, she was also capable of giving a lot of pleasure in reward. Finally, I settled on a long-sleeved vest in very sheer net. Beneath it, I wore a tight pair of PVC shorts and black patent sixteen-hole Doctor Martens. I inserted my rings into my nipple piercings, hoping that this would attract curious and admiring gazes. I left my waist-length blond hair loose, and made my face up carefully, emphasising my full lips and big, green eyes. When Greg and Anna turned up to collect me, I could see from the expression on their faces that they had made the right choice.

'You look hard and soft at the same time,' Anna told me. 'Maura will be wet as anything the moment she sees you.'

Jon and Maura owned a big, three-storey Victorian house, the only one in its road not to be converted into flats, or so it seemed. When I asked Anna what the couple did for a living she said that Jon was a lawyer who specialised in corporate cases, and Maura was a television producer. That explained their lavish lifestyle.

The house itself was beautiful, Jon and Maura holding court in the living room. He was in his forties with steel-grey hair and piercing blue eyes, while red-haired Maura was as tall and slender as a supermodel. There was a cold buffet spread out on the table, and the two dozen or so guests were encouraged to help themselves to food and drink. I could not help but notice a couple of bowls of condoms, of all colours and textures, it seemed, sitting on the coffee table; the couple had thought of everything.

It was hard to pinpoint exactly when the small-talk stopped and events moved on to a more serious level. At first, it was nothing more than a caress of a breast or a buttock as people talked to each other I soon noticed that one girl had removed her top and was allowing her male partner to suckle nipples, while another was down on vigorously sucking the penis of her partner. His hands were on the top of forcing her firmly into his groin, and I marvelled at the ease at which she was taking what must have a good seven inches of rigid cock flesh down her throat.

'Why don't we see what's under those little shorts of yours, eh?' a soft, Scottish-accented voice whispered in my ear, and I realised with a start it was Maura speaking. Without waiting for an answer from me, she rapidly unzipped my shorts and pulled them down my legs. She smiled in approval at the sight of my freshly shaven cock and balls. 'Mouthwatering, my dear, simply mouthwatering,' she said with a smile, and ran a hand casually over my ass-cheeks, as if checking how spankable they were.

I looked round frantically, trying to spot Greg and Anna, but they were nowhere to be seen. Jon had mentioned when we arrived that most of the action would be taking place in the playroom, and I wondered if the two of them had gone there. I was aware that heads had turned, watching as Maura played with me as though I was her latest toy. I had not expected to be the centre of attention so soon, and I was excited and frightened by the thought of what might be about to happen.

'You mustn't come without my permission,' Maura warned me, as her hand moved faster. Her thumb and forefinger closed around my shaft, bringing my cock to full erection. She knew exactly what she was doing, and I was fighting hard against the orgasmic sensations which were beginning to build somewhere deep within my balls. I was afraid that if I came before she let me, she would punish me, and even as I strove to avoid giving her that satisfaction, the pleasure became too much. I groaned as a finger stroked unerringly over my glans as the other hand fellated my cock, until I spattered the mesh of my vest with my come, while the remainder dribbled down the length of my shaft.

Maura's soft tones became a threatening growl. 'You were warned, slave,' she said, and grabbed hold of my wrist. I was dragged out of the living room, leaving my shorts forgotten on the deep-pile carpet, my boots clomping on the polished wooden floorboards in the hall. I was dimly aware that several of the people who had been watching Maura wank me were following us, and I knew that they would all take great pleasure in seeing the mistress of the house give me whatever punishment was my due.

As I had suspected, Greg and Anna were in the playroom when we got there. Greg was chained facing the black-painted wall, and Anna was taking a short, many-tailed whip to his backside. Fresh weals joined those that already marked his skin. It was clear they had been there for some while. Anna stopped what she was doing as Maura and I arrived. 'When you bring guests, I expect they are told the rules,' Maura explained to a smiling Anna. 'I told this weak-willed worm he wasn't allowed to come and yet he creamed himself all over my hand, like the disobedient little whelp he is. I think the only punishment is a taste of my whip.'

Ignoring the protests I was making, Maura bent me over a padded whipping horse which was in the middle of the playroom. While Anna watched, she pushed my legs apart and secured them in a spreader bar, then she fastened my wrists on the far side of the whipping horse. Satisfied she could not move, she took down an evil-looking cat with three short, plaited tails from a rack of implements. Giving me no time to prepare myself, she brought it down hard on my cheeks, the thin net material which covered them offering scant protection. I, however, could do nothing to prevent her slashing the instrument across my buttocks again and again. At last, she tired of punishing me, and came around to stand in front of me. She smoothed away a lock of my hair from where it was clinging to my tear-stained face, and told me I had taken the punishment well. She then announced that I was available to whoever wished to use me.

For the next hour or so, I was at the mercy of Maura, Jon and their guests. I was fucked by a succession of condom-clad cocks, including, I was sure from the feel, at least one strap-on. My ass was toyed with repeatedly, while I moaned and writhed, pressing my cock hard against the padded top of the whipping horse to give it the stimulation it craved. Then I was freed and ordered to pleasure Maura and Anna orally in turn, my tongue working overtime as I sought to bring each of them to orgasm. Finally, I was sucked by Jon as I lay on the floor with Maura squatting over my mouth, urging me to lick her. When she came, she peed over my face in her excitement – a first for me. At last, I was allowed the privilege of showering in the couple's en-suite bathroom, to wash the semen, sweat and love juice from my exhausted body. Next time I go, I won't be the new kid on the block and, hopefully, I will get the chance to watch someone else endure the pain and wonderful pleasure I experienced that night.

* * *

They've banned them now, but I used to love it when London was full of those fliers in phoneboxes. They'd advertise stuff you hadn't even thought of before, like electrical play, or else they'd be some cheesy money-for-nothing thing like 'nanny forces you to sit in her pee'. It used to tickle me pink to think that anyone who wanted to make a call – and these days now everyone has mobiles that's usually tourists – was confronted by offers plastered to the wall. You might be frantically calling round hotels to find a room, juggling change, knowing you'd be OK if only you wanted some bizarre sexual service and not just a common-or-garden bed for the night.

But more than this, I loved them because they started off my favourite fantasy. I imagine that I make regular visits to my mistress. She is my goddess, and it is an honour and a privilege to serve her. She knows my worthless body is hers to do with as she wishes, and I will bear whatever torments she inflicts upon me without complaint.

My mistress is a trained beautician, and she uses her skills to torture me in the most exquisite ways. Once a month, I am compelled to visit her at her salon, after all her clients have gone, for my regular routine. She demands that I keep my body completely free of hair, and to aid me in this process she will wax me. I cannot describe the agonies I undergo as she paints the hot wax over my chest, limbs and genitals, before swiftly and ruthlessly ripping it away. The sensation of my pubic hair being pulled out by the roots is one that brings tears to my eyes, but I must bear it in silence or risk her wrath. Next, she will give me an enema. The nozzle is greased and inserted into my anus with ease, then I am made to take up to two pints of water at blood temperature. Soon, my bowels are churning and I am begging for relief, but she will not stop until I have taken every last drop. I am not allowed any dignity, for she will watch as I evacuate the water into a chamber pot. Once she is sure that I am completely cleansed, she will strap me to the table on which her clients receive their treatments, using wide brown leather straps – real heavy old hospital ones, all creased with use – which are surprisingly strong and hold me securely in place. Then she will use one of her machines on me, all of which are capable of producing electric shocks which vary in severity. Her favourite is the slimming device, which consists of a number of small pads, designed to be attached to whichever part of the body is in need of toning and firming. I never need to ask where these pads will be applied in my case, for I know it will be my penis. Once they are secured in place, she will turn the machine to its lowest setting, the electricity stimulating my poor, tormented cock in ways that are both painful and yet deliciously arousing. I know she takes pleasure in the sight of my body twitching and writhing in its bonds, and her sublime cruelty only serves to turn me on further. I would dread my visits to my mistress in reality I think, although rationally I know I should try it. You're a long time dead, and it *would* be just like the fantasy – I could direct the action after all, instructing her to finally allow me the ultimate release of orgasm.

6

TV Eye

Corsets, sheer denier, and the bi-curious

- 'We may protest that "the pervert is always someone else!" But our fantasies betray our hypocrisy.
  What is a "normal" erotic fantasy? Fantasy, or
  imagination, is inevitably about the forbidden and
  the impossible.'[1]

Recently, my wife's been promoted at work and this
has been accompanied by her being required to go
overseas on a few business trips. As her mother lives
with us since she's been a widow, and it's just been
me and her in the house on these occasions, this has
led to some rather curious fantasies on my part. For
some spurious reason, I imagine my mother-in-law is
an aunt or governess who's called upon to feminise
and spank me to teach me a lesson. She finds me
entirely co-operative as she has some means to
blackmail me, say. This accounts for how a relatively
infirm woman like her can have a 45-year-old ex-
rugby forward like me in her thrall. For starters, she

---

[1] *Fetish: Fashion, Sex and Power*, Valerie Steele, OUP 1996

dresses me in frilly, satiny little-girl clothes until I am completely humiliated. She spanks me with her hand, over her knee, until her hand hurts as much as my poor bottom, then binds me hand and foot with ribbons and makes me stand in a dark cupboard with the door closed, to concentrate on my poor painful bottom, and will not let me out until tea-time. If I make a sound, she's told me, she'll gag me with a pair of her old directoire knickers. But how can I tell her I need to wee wee? Eventually I can hold it no longer, and it soaks from my penis out through the satiny clothes. Now I can only wait, imagining how cross Auntie will be at tea-time!

When Auntie opens the door, a shaft of light blinds me as I hear her sniff the air. My punishment is severe – I'm made to bend over the back of the settee, and take six from her tawse on my satin-clad behind. As I wiggle my hips in frightened anticipation, and with each merciless stroke, my penis is pushed against the back of the sofa until I can't ignore the stimulation. She had undone my bindings in order to drag me over to the settee, and now I rub sore bottom cheeks in shame, betraying, as I stand, how my cock is aching to get out of the satin, pulling it tight at the seams. She feeds me a little and although it is only tea-time, tells me it is my supper, and that I'm to go straight to bed for being a bad little girl. Because I obviously can't control myself, and because I've just drunk tea, I'm an accident waiting to happen, and clearly I'll have to wear nappies to bed. Up in the nursery, Auntie talcs me and wanks me off, telling me how good I've been to take my punishment without protest. When I come, she briskly folds the nappy over my wilting penis and my messy spend, and fastens it. When my wife returns from her trip, she finds me sitting up in bed while Auntie reads me a bedtime story, telling me over and over how pretty I look as a little girl. In my fantasy I do hope she has to go away on business again soon, so I can be looked after by my stern but loving babysitter.

* * *

I love going to fetish clubs, because you never know what might happen to you or just who you might meet. Take a recent example. I was at a popular club on the London scene, when I spotted a beautiful woman ordering a drink at the bar. Now, I am not particularly into playing a dominant or submissive role, I just like to meet other people who enjoy dressing for pleasure, and it was obvious from the moment I saw her that she did. She was wearing a red, long-sleeved rubber dress that clung erotically to her small breasts and slim hips, fishnet stockings the tops of which were just visible beneath the hem of the dress, and red patent stiletto-heeled shoes which boosted her already impressive height to well over six feet. Her long, black hair fell in a shining wave to waist length, and her make-up was immaculate. It was lust at first sight, so I went over and introduced myself.

She told me in husky tones that her name was Simone, and when I offered to pay for her vodka and tonic she accepted graciously. As we chatted, we seemed to have so much in common that I sensed some hot sex was on the cards. After all, people reckon I am pretty good-looking, with my closely cropped peroxide blond hair and muscular body, and I got the impression Simone liked what she saw. That impression was confirmed when, after a couple of drinks, she suggested we go somewhere to get to know each other a little better. I wanted to know what she had in mind, and she asked how I felt about a quick fuck in the toilets? I was a little taken aback, I have to admit, as she seemed much more forward than some of the other women I have met on the scene, but I would have been lying if I said my cock did not twitch in my pants at her suggestion. We headed for the ladies', nobody turning a hair as we squeezed in one of the cubicles together. It's pretty much a given that someone will end up screwing in the loos before the end of the evening at one of these places, and as long as you don't hog a cubicle when there is a queue you can usually get away with it. It also goes without saying that the ladies' is always more salubrious than the gents'. When the door was safely locked behind us, I urged Simone to push her dress up towards her waist and pull down her panties, and that was when I got a massive shock. For there, tucked out of the way, was what was unmistakably a penis. Simone was not what she seemed – in fact, she was Simon.

My mouth gaped open for a split second, and then I thought, What the hell? As Simone brought her cock out of its hiding place and began to stroke it, I dropped to my knees and took it between my lips. It tasted warm and salty, and not at all unpleasant, and as it expanded in my mouth to its full six inches I fell to my task with relish. Simone was moaning, urging me on, her hands with their false red nails raking my scalp as I sucked away. The backdrop to what we were doing must have been acting as a powerful turn-on for Simone, because, sooner than I might have expected, she was coming, her spunk hitting the back of my throat in a series of powerful jets.

Then she turned round, and offered me her ass. My cock was aching for relief, so I freed my leather jeans and told Simone to grab hold of the toilet cistern. She wriggled her backside at me, squealing out loud as I eased my dick up her with a hastily applied condom. The novelty of fucking a transvestite in the toilets of a fetish club, knowing anyone outside would be aware of exactly what were doing from the noises we were making, excited me beyond belief, and I came as quickly as she had done. When we came out of the cubicle, a couple of girls looked at us and winked at Simone, as taken in by her authentically feminine appearance as I had been. If only you knew, I thought, as we went to get a well-earned drink.

* * *

I used to work with a girl, Sam, who took a shine to me. Fortunately, we weren't in the same department, or even on the same floor. She wasn't that smart I suppose but she was somehow enigmatic. It helped that she was a tall, willowy blonde with a nice smile too I suppose! Anyway, she was coming on all adventurous to me one evening in the pub. It was a leaving party for someone we all liked who was changing jobs and, as these things do sometimes, it had a wistful air, and it was getting towards closing, even with the extended bar hours the company had worked out with the pub. I should explain that I'm an in-house photographer with a design company, and sometimes I get to go on photoshoots which sound glamorous, with beautiful models and interesting locations, but in reality of course are sheer hard work and take a lot of organisation. Nevertheless, she was asking me all these suggestive questions about sex with models, if I'd ever done glamour work, that kind of thing. One second I was smelling the rum and coke on her breath and she was asking me if I'd consider taking some glamour shots of her, nothing serious . . . and the next her tongue was in the back of my throat. Somehow, in the haze of drink, I'd lost track of how it got there.

We reeled outside, and carried on snogging outside the door of the pub, probably causing a few tongues to wag given how bored work people get, not that we weren't both single. I remember there was an iron-barred gate where they must have rolled the kegs in and I held her arms up and pushed her against it, letting her feel my hard-on against her pubis and taking my turn to bury my tongue deep into her mouth. After chatting for a bit, during which we groped and kissed some more, we went back and joined the thinning crew of drinkers. At that point Laurence, an outrageously camp and really quite lovable black guy who worked on reception, whom I'd been chatting to earlier, engaged me in conversation again. I don't know if Laurence feels he has to play to the gallery. He's an intelligent guy but he never gives up with the innuendo. The three of us left at the same time, and as we walked to the tube station, I was in the middle, carrying on two conversations, as a light drizzle hit our faces, waking us up. On the one hand I had Laurence telling me I was bi and that if I didn't think I was well couldn't I just pretend he was a woman? Meanwhile, Sam and I were establishing that we lived on different sides of the city, and that for one reason or another, the moment – for that night at least – had gone. All the while I was watching her pert, perky tits bounce lightly as she walked, the wind blowing her coat open, and she drunkenly, pleasantly weaving and leaning into me for support.

Anyway, I had to be up early, and would rather have had one off the wrist at the thought of what might have happened with Sam than start experimenting with Laurence, as I wasn't that drunk. I wish now, it had been a Friday night, I'd had some coke and drink back at the flat, and none of us had to do anything the next day. Perhaps I would have had the guts to take charge and say, 'come on you two, cab back to mine.' I've thought since how much I would have liked to see Laurence's puckered asshole winking at me as Sam wanked herself for my arousal, or else took Laurence's cock to see if she could 'turn' him. I've begun to imagine how my white hot spunk might have looked streaked across Laurence's smooth Nubian backside, how tight he would be next to what I'm used to, no disrespect. I wonder what it would be like to be given head – as I go down on Sam – by someone who also knows what it's like to have a cock and have it stimulated. I wonder what it would be like to take *his* hard, rubbery shaft into *my* throat. And I'm sure Laurence would find it in himself to help me out with Sam, maybe taking her in the ass as I'm in front, both of us lifting her between us, feeling our cocks rub together through her membraneous insides, sending her into orgasms which make her shake her blonde tresses in release. Most of all perhaps, I'd like to wank off as I watched Laurence and Sam together, her blue-eyed, blonde beauty and his Masai elegance and velvet-skinned good looks. The possibilities are endless.

* * *

My fantasy has always been to serve two equally dominant mistresses, and to be made to do whatever they require of me, no matter how difficult or demeaning. I see myself becoming a full-time slave to the pair, being forced to relinquish my job and to hand over all my assets, including my house, my car and the contents of my bank account, to them. As I am to become their maid, they dispose of my male clothing, and make me wear nothing but a little frilly white apron and a collar round my neck which marks me as their property. My male name is relinquished and I become known to them as Snowdrop. From the moment they wake to the moment they retire to bed, I am at the mercy of their every whim and command. I sleep in the kitchen, chained by my collar to the pipes beneath the sink, so that I am ready to prepare their breakfast as soon as they wake me by ringing the bell they keep beside their beds. I have to perform all the household chores: I dust the house from top to bottom, I keep the kitchen spotlessly clean, I do the ironing and I wash my mistresses' clothes. Their expensive silk and lace lingerie has to be handwashed, and woe betide me if I am caught taking a surreptitious sniff of their feminine aromas from the gussets of their panties! Their standards of cleanliness are exactingly high, and if I slack in any respect – from leaving the smallest smear on the dressing table mirror to neglecting to clean behind the cooker – I am soundly thrashed as a reminder not to do it again.

I am also required to attend to my mistresses' sexual needs. Normally, they will torment me by offering me the merest glimpse up their long, stocking-clad legs when I am kneeling at their feet. Mistress Tania, in particular, delights in standing above me wearing no panties, allowing me to gaze up at her beautiful blonde bush and the shell-pink folds of her sex lips. I am not allowed to get an erection without permission, but the sight of Mistress Tania's glorious cunt is usually too much for me, and she will punish me for my gross impertinence by slapping my erect penis with her gloved hand. However, I am occasionally ordered to pleasure my mistresses orally, and I find it such an honour to lick and lap at their beautiful pussies and succulent clits until they climax. Of course, I am not permitted any relief myself at these times, and before I begin I am strapped into a severe penis restraint with spikes on the inside, which prick my sensitive cock flesh as soon as it begins to rise. Sometimes, my mistresses will take pity on me and allow me to wank myself until I come; my hand shuttles up and down my shaft to the accompaniment of jeers of derision from my mistresses and comments about the puny size of my prick. When finally my semen oozes out over my fist, they just laugh and tell me to go and clean myself up.

The highlight of my existence is when Mistress Tania and Mistress Dionne decide to throw a party, to which they will invite all their equally dominant friends. Then, I can look forward to being at the mercy of as many as a dozen cruel, stunningly attractive women, all of whom know that they have carte blanche to do with me as they will. On these special occasions, my shoulder-length red hair is put into two bunches, which are tied with pink ribbon. A third piece of ribbon is tied around my cock, and when ordered to, I must raise my apron to show my pink bow to everyone in the room. As you can imagine, my attire causes hoots of laughter from the assembled guests and comments about what a pretty little sissy I am. I spend the evening attending to the guests, whatever way they desire. I move between them with glasses of champagne and canapés, to the accompaniment of hands reaching under my little frills to fondle my cock and balls. I cannot prevent myself from getting an erection with this constant attention, even though I know it is expressly forbidden, and when Mistress Tania spots my hard cock against the apron, she orders the entertainment to begin.

I am taken to the centre of the room, and made to bend over the back of a chair, my hairy ass exposed to the gaze of all the women. Mistress Dionne brings out two dice and announces that throwing the first one will determine the particular implement I'm given my strokes with, and the second determines what the count will be. One is the hand, two is the hairbrush, three is the riding crop, four is the cat-o'-nine-tails, five is the tawse and six is my least favourite, the thin, whippy cane. As you can imagine, the chances of anyone throwing a double six or indeed a six of any particular punishment adds considerably to my dread and the glee of my mistresses, who are always the last to take their turns. By the time they do, my backside is a mass of pain, my flesh scarlet marked with vicious raised weals where the cane has left its mark or my skin has been caught by the tails of the tawse. However, my mistresses show me no pity, and lay on their allotted instruments with all the severity they can muster. If all they are to give is a hand spanking, they will wet their palms to make the slaps more painful for me. Sometimes I will be made to complete my humiliation by thanking each of my punishers on bended knee.

* * *

I have been brought to the sumptuous home of a friend of my sissy mistress, Guy, at my mistress's insistence, and I am standing before him. I have caramel-coloured skin and long, straight dark hair. My breasts are very firm and full, thanks to a course of hormones, and appear even larger due to the fact that my waist is tiny and my hips flare out beneath it thanks to a strict regime of corsetry. I was aware of Guy walking all the way round me, but I did not dare

raise my gaze to his. 'How did she behave in the car?'
I heard him asking the chauffeur.

'Just as she was asked to,' the chauffeur replied.
'It's a pity you didn't ask me to fuck her,' he added
ruefully.

'All in good time,' Guy said. 'I can promise you
that you will have your fill of her cock and ass before
she leaves here.' I shivered at the casual way in which
I was being discussed, though in truth the slim,
dark-haired chauffeur was almost as good-looking as
my master, and the prospect of him fucking me, even
in my tight anus, was not an unpleasant one. I felt
Guy's hand on the point of my chin and he raised my
face so I was staring into his warm green eyes.

'You have been prepared something to eat,' Guy
said. 'I'll take you into the kitchen.' He led me down
the hallway and into the kitchen as I stumbled and
hobbled like the sissy I was, struggling to keep up in
my four-inch heels. I looked around for other members of his staff, but saw no one. 'I only employ
Mayfield, the chauffeur, and Christie. She's the cook
and housekeeper. She's for the night but you'll meet
her tomorrow. The food is keeping warm in the stove.
Take it out.'

I retrieved a plate of delicious-smelling stew and
went to take it to the kitchen table, but Guy stopped
me. 'No, you stupid slut,' he said curtly. 'On the
floor!' I realised there was a metal ring set in the
skirting board close to the cooker. As I watched, Guy
retrieved a length of chain from a cupboard, along
with a wide leather collar that had a D-ring at the
front. He fastened the collar tightly round my neck.
'While you're here, you will wear this at all times, to
show that you are my property, albeit temporarily.
He attached the chain to the ring in the collar, then
secured the other end to the ring in the skirting

board. Then he took the plate from my hands and placed it on the floor. 'Eat,' he ordered.

With no cutlery offered or asked for, I got on my knees and ate my dinner like a dog. The stew tasted as good as it smelled, but that did not lessen the indignity of my position. My sissy mistress companion had never yet treated me like this, and now I realised why she thought a couple of days under the scrutiny of Guy would teach me to better understand the reality of servitude. After I had licked the plate completely clean, Guy unclipped my chain from the wall, and took me to my bedroom. By now, it was nearly eleven o'clock. 'You will be sleeping on the floor tonight,' he told me. 'If I wake you at any point and demand sexual relief from you, you will not refuse. If you behave and do everything I ask, you will be allowed to sleep on the bed tomorrow night.' With that, he began to undress, finally slipping between the sheets naked, while I curled up in a ball on the floor and did my best to fall asleep. It was difficult; although the room was not cold, I missed the comfort of a blanket to pull over myself, and images were running through my head of Guy waking with an erection, which he would order me to suck or take in my compliant ass. Eventually, I drifted off, and was almost disappointed that Guy decided against using me during the course of the night.

In the morning, I was woken by a woman coming into the room carrying a tray. Grey-haired and in her fifties, she must have been the housekeeper, Mrs Christie. She set Guy's breakfast down in front of him as he sat up in bed, but I noticed there was no food for me. 'You'll be eating in the kitchen again,' Guy told me. 'But first you have to use the toilet. Mrs Christie will supervise you.' The housekeeper un-chained me from the foot of the bed and led me into

Guy's en-suite bathroom. I expected her to shut the door and leave me privacy, but she just stood there, arms folded.

'Master has asked me to make sure you do as you are told,' she said. Her tone was not unfriendly. Previously I had peed only under the gaze of my own companion. I had never had anyone else watch me perform such an intimate task. I sat on the toilet and voided my bladder with difficulty as Mrs Christie stood there. When I had finished, she tore a couple of sheets of toilet roll, ordered me to open my legs wide and wiped my ass and powdered it dispassionately, adding to my humiliation. Then she took me off to the kitchen to have a snack which, as before, I had to eat on all fours.

After breakfast, Guy decided to introduce me to some of the implements at his disposal. He took me down to a dungeon which he had had installed in his cellar, and I was going to learn what it was really like being punished. He had a large and generously padded stool, over which I was told to bend. Once I was in place, he chained my wrists and ankles to the stool. My legs were widely spread apart, which would give Guy access to my balls and anus. I shuddered at the thought of those knowing green eyes scrutinising my smoothened perineum and puckered brown-eye. 'A few with the whip first, I think,' he murmured. Chained as I was, I could not see what type of whip he was referring to; it could have been anything from a short riding whip to a full-blooded bullwhip. However, when I felt him trailing the instrument over my backside and down the cleft between my cheeks, I realised it had many short, soft leather tails, and realised he was going to use this to soften me up before applying something more severe to my behind.

I tensed, waiting for him to lay it on. The anticipation was causing me to tremble in my restraints, yet I would be lying if I said that was purely through fear. I dreaded the punishment he was about to inflict on me, true, but I also welcomed it. The discipline I had already received at the hands of my companion – limited though it was turning out to have been – had taught me there was a point where pain and pleasure blurred and became one, and I was sure Guy would know exactly how to take me to that place. I heard the tails of the whip whistling through the air and then they landed, spreading out across the surface of my rear, each tip prickling me with a little sting of discomfort. He knew what he was doing, and his swift, methodical strokes were covering every inch of skin, moving down to stripe the soft flesh of my inner thighs. I moaned and wriggled in my bonds, but in truth I was in no real pain. Instead, I was reacting to the engorged feeling of my cock and the growing awareness of my whole sensualised body. I could smell my own sweat in the closed confines of the dungeon.

At last, he threw down the whip and went to choose another implement. This time, he walked in front of me as he returned to the whipping stool, allowing me to get a clear view of what he was holding. It was a tawse. My sissy mistress had never used the instrument on me, but I knew of the vicious instrument by reputation. A tawse was designed with two tails, so that when they landed on your skin, they would pinch a bit of it painfully between the tails. This was going to hurt far more than the whip, and I held my breath as Guy came to stand behind me once more. He slapped the tawse against my pain, and I shuddered, knowing that he was just prolonging my agony. I wanted this to be over and done with, but he took his time. He was just as thorough with the tawse as he had been with the whip, only this time the pain was much more severe. I could not stop myself from yelling as the rough leather straps landed on my bum. Shock radiated out until my whole ass was throbbing. I could feel tears pricking my eyes. Guy ran his fingers over the ridges the tawse raised on my skin. Even though his touch was gentler, I could not stop myself from wincing and trying to pull away.

'Have you had enough, slut?' he asked me, and I nodded, even though I knew that would only encourage him to punish me even further. But, to my surprise and gratitude, he unshackled me and let me stretch my cramped limbs. Then he led me back to the kitchen and chained me up again.

I must have fallen asleep, because the next thing I knew was a gentle kick in my ribs. I jerked awake to see Mayfield, the chauffeur, staring down at me with a grin on his face. I must have looked wretched, face still blotchy with tears and my bum bearing marks of the tawse, and I wondered what was to happen. He quickly unfastened me, and led me to the garden. Guy was sitting in a deckchair drinking a glass of Pimm's, and he nodded his approval at the sight of me, naked and standing meekly before him, my cock half-erect and bobbing before me.

'Fetch Mrs Christie,' Guy told my chauffeur. 'I want you both here for this.' I wanted to ask what his intention was, but dared not. I soon found out, as Mrs Christie joined us on the lawn, wiping her hands on her apron. 'I want you both to see how obedient the little slut is,' he told them. Then he turned his attention to me and I realised he was loosing his cock from his flies. 'On your knees and suck, slut.' I could no more have dreamed of disobeying him than I could of flying to the moon. I opened my lips and took the mushroom head of his dick between them.

He tasted warm and salty and I licked him with relish, oblivious to the fact that I was being watched by his domestic staff. I was expecting him to come in my mouth, but after a few minutes he pulled out, turning to Mayfield. 'She's good,' he said, 'but don't take my word for it. See for yourself.'

The chauffeur smiled and dropped his uniform trousers. My jaw dropped at the size of his cock, and my own humble measure twitched. Even flaccid, the chauffeur's was longer than his boss's, and I doubted for a moment whether I would be able to wrap my lips around it. I had no time to ponder that, as he thrust it roughly into my mouth. It hardened rapidly as I began to suck it, and soon I was almost choking on the solid column of flesh that pressed against my palate. Unlike Guy, he didn't withdraw when he sensed he was coming, and I spluttered as a hot jet of spunk hit the back of my throat. I did my best to swallow it down, my eyes watering as I struggled to cope. I could feel Guy's mocking gaze on me, and felt inadequate and humiliated.

That was nothing, however, to what I felt a moment later, as Mayfield withdrew his shrinking manhood from my mouth, and wiped it clean on my hair. Guy was gesturing to Mrs Christie. 'We've seen what she can do with a cock,' he said. 'Now let's see what she's like with a pussy.' This was not something I had expected, and I tried to object as the house-keeper lifted her skirts to reveal that she wore no knickers. I stared at the crinkled, grey hair that covered her cunt, and realised there was no way I could back out. As she pushed me down on to the grass and settled herself over my face, my nostrils were assailed with her ripe, tangy odour. Afraid of what Guy might do to me if I didn't comply, I reached out my tongue and began to run it along her slit.

Mrs Christie was a heavy woman, and she was pressing me into the grass as she writhed on my face. Her juices were starting to flow into my face as I lapped at her pussy, and I was aware of Guy and his chauffeur commenting on my performance, as I did my best to satisfy her. I found her clitoris and stabbed at it with my tongue trying to pleasure her in the way I imagined she would have liked to be pleasured. Sighs of enjoyment and the way she ground her cunt against my nose indicated that I must be doing something right. Suddenly, she gave a harsh cry. I realised she was coming, her thigh muscles holding me in such a tight grasp that I feared I would suffocate, unable to breathe in anything but gushing, matronly come. At last, she released her grip on me and I rolled from under her, gasping for breath like a landed fish and with Guy's mocking laughter ringing in my ears. I sensed, though, that I had passed a test, however inexpertly, and knew that I'd be returned to my sissy mistress with a good report card.

I passed the rest of the weekend in similar fashion, alternating between being kept restrained in some part of Guy's house and being asked to show my sexual devotion to him and his staff. Both Mayfield and Mrs Christie fucked me repeatedly, the housekeeper using a strap-on dildo of absorbable proportions, which I was ordered to moisten with lube before she thrust it into me, and to lick it clean of my ass-tang when she had finished.

On the Sunday before I left, Guy chose to give me a goodbye treat. I could feel my stomach muscles clenching in sick anticipation as I watched Guy grease his erect cock with the clear lubricating gel. To add to my degradation, he told Mrs Christie to hold me in place as he buggered me. The housekeeper had stripped to the waist, revealing her huge, pendulous breasts with their rubbery red nipples, and my face was crushed between them as I felt Guy kicking my legs wide apart before placing the head of his cock at the entrance to my anus. I did my best to relax as he began to push his way through my anal ring, everting my muscle to receive him. To stifle my sissy yelps, Mrs Christie unceremoniously stuffed one of her nipples into my mouth and ordered me to suck. I did as I was told, chewing on her stiff teat as Guy thrust into my ass with increasing ferocity. It seemed to take for ever before I felt my shaft grow even bigger and thicker in the brief moment before he pumped his spunk into the condom, deep within my body. At last, he pulled out of me and whipped off the latex sheath, wiping his cock clean on my face before hauling me back into the kitchen and chaining me up until it was time for me to leave.

I was finally returned to my mistress, weary and still frustrated but knowing I had passed every ordeal Guy had put me through. I have been warned that if I fall from the high standards of sissy housework that are expected of me, I will be sent back for another weekend, and I have to admit that on one level I am almost looking forward to it.

* * *

Minor fantasies, or some of them: aged twenty or so, masturbating a male friend, having him do so to me; aged fifty masturbating a younger man, tall, strong and muscular, perhaps black; sunbathing naked with a female friend who will not mind if I have an erection (come to think of it I have done that); remembering swimming naked rather than doing it, which after the first though very beautiful moments turned out to be much like swimming with a costume; swimming naked with an erection which I have done once, like fucking the sea. I'm not much interested in supposedly sexy costumes and revolted by anything to do with assholes, but what was hinted at in the Stephen Fry film about Oscar Wilde where they were face to face, rubbing erections together? Don't think I would enjoy that much but I'd like to try it once. I've several times (but can never quite remember it) had sex in a posture I've never seen in any book, so that my testicles can be played with at the same time. I think some of the postures I've seen in pictures look uncomfortable or impossible. Other fantasies: a woman with auburn hair, blue eyes, pale skin, a brunette ditto, a woman with a great deal of chestnut pubic hair, yoga teachers, gym mistresses, hockey players.

8

Auto-Erotica

DIY tips!

Sting in the Tail
I play with myself sometimes – play? no, it's worth taking seriously – according to the penis-strengthening exercises in a book on tantric yoga I have – finishing by holding the erection lightly at the top with one hand, stroking it with the other twenty times, then nineteen and so on down to one. The book says start with ten.

* * *

I'm prompted by your survey to tell you, also, about my method of wanking. I switch the tape recorder to record and then describe my actions while I tug at my cock. I comment on how I am rubbing my prick and then when I am ready to come I pull my legs over my head and rest my feet on the settee so that my prick is pointing down towards my mouth.

I then rub slowly until I come, and as my hot salty fluid shoots into my mouth and on my face I make sure that I can be heard licking and swallowing. Later

I play the recording to my girlfriend who thinks it's great. She listens intently to all the details, especially when I come. My girlfriend always likes to watch me come and her favourite method is to get me to lie in bed and to pull my feet over my head and rest them on the headboard. She then kneels down on the bed so that she can look down between my legs and at my cock pointing towards my mouth. She rubs my prick with her right hand and opens my mouth with her left. She masturbates me slowly and when I reach a peak she aims my come into my mouth. She wanks me until she's milked the last drop, and she really enjoys watching. 'Now you know how horrible it tastes!' she says.

I am very much into my girlfriend's underwear. Whenever my girlfriend goes out for the evening, I go upstairs to our bedroom, close the curtains and start my private act. Firstly I arrange the mirrors to get the best view of my performance, then I do a striptease show in front of them, which brings on a huge erection. Selecting the most sexy pair of undies from my girlfriend's collection, I pull them up over my crotch and try to contain my prick and balls inside them. This is usually quite difficult, as my balls keep popping out of the sides, and my prick bursts over the top which I like. I get so excited by the reflections of myself in mirrors in this state of sexual ecstasy, that my very moist end starts dribbling. When I can stand the suspense no longer, I wank myself off and close the door.

* * *

My girlfriend really enjoys reading magazines before we screw, and they always makes her especially randy. I always know when she's in the mood for a good fucking because when we go past a newsagents she'll glance up at the sex literature. Usually she lets me do the buying, but if it's a female shop assistant Tracey's not averse to buying them herself.

If we're both feeling horny when we're hanging out, we'll have a little excitement, and, if it's sunny, we'll go to the park, giving Tracey a chance for a little exhibitionism. Tracey finds a potential audience – not hard for a pretty, slutty girl like her, and sits facing him with her legs apart, her knickers on full view and her skirt rucked up a bit more towards her waist, crossing and uncrossing her legs. She calls this the Sharon Stone. She always does it so as to appear totally casual, since this adds to her excitement. She always leaves a great deal of unshaven hair around her cunt so as to present a really stimulating sight and generally wears small, pale-coloured panties which cling more and more tightly to her cunt lips as her vaginal juices start to flow. Her mound and clit are quite pronounced, which really gets to me, and are quite visible once the sticky wet patch has started to appear! At this point we usually end up tongue-kissing and stroking each other. I often can't resist running my hand up Tracey's thighs and tracing the outline of her hole – an act that is invariably appreciated by spectators. By this stage it's time to go back to mine.

Once home Tracey has been known to grab the dirty mag, face-down on the hearth-rug, her right hand at her fanny, desperate to relieve herself. She never undresses, finding it 'dirtier' to wank fully clothed. Tracey always loves it if I stand and ejaculate over her. She likes to rub my semen into her dress, T-shirt and hair. Although my passion usually subsides for a time after this, Tracey is just starting, and after a while her moans and obscenities have me worked up again. She loves me to do things that some people would consider distasteful. I'll take off her knickers and smell and suck the juice-stained crotch, all the time masturbating for her benefit and she finds my habit of licking the hairy area around her anus really exciting. She loves to rim me and once she used her small vibrator on her ass and then licked it clean in front of me. She likes me to leave conspicuous love-bites on her neck and breasts and she finds the subsequent randy looks she gets from male customers in the shop where she works a real turn-on. Tracey tells me that she often has to slope off to the staff toilet and have a quick wank so as to relieve the tension.

I never thought that a common-or-garden porn mag would stimulate me more than anything else apart from the real thing, but I get such wild fantasies just from looking at the models, all of whom are each a month's supply of tossing-off material in themselves. Sad to say, I occasionally mumble away to the girls' pictures and what they are missing by not being at this address. But the most sexy ideas come out as I look at the really dirty, slutty wives at the end of certain of the magazines. This is because they are clearly less bored with having their cunts photographed, and seem to be enjoying the fun, much more if their 'come on' expressions are anything to go by. Those expressions often get come on in a different way.

Once in a while one will stand out, as it were, and I'll make a note of where I've put her, turn her corners down. One recent model is very special to me not only because of the very knowing dirty smile she produces in the first picture of the shoot, but also owing to a pair of amazing tits and a truly astonishing cunt that hasn't yet failed to induce a regular and massive erection. Men boast about the size of their pricks and women fantasise about gigantic spunk-spurters, but it was not until I had studied Jinny's hole that my astonishment and interest in cunt measurements arose.

The actual length from high up in her pubes to its end, well back in her crotch, must be all of ten inches. If the length bow to stern bears any relationship to its capacity I would reckon she could accommodate anything and anybody and still have room to spare. It certainly exceeds anything I have ever come across – or in. Of course, I would dearly love to see it in its hairy, fleshy and moist magnificence, but all I am able to do is to return to her picture and continue to marvel and fantasise. This I have done on many occasions, and she is by my side as I write.

When I've finished I shall, as usual, deflate the very hard cock I now have in the best way I know how, taking care not to spill any on Jinny. I hope Jinny would be flattered if she knew that since February when she first came into my life I have used her exclusively for wanking and have shot my load looking at her incredible cunt on around fifty occasions.

* * *

I have tried various ways of wanking whilst looking at the pin-ups in my favourite porn mags, but it is very difficult to hold the page open with one hand, since one needs a third hand with a tissue to catch the sperm – otherwise it shoots all over the pages with sticky consequences. I have tried using a condom, but find that this comes off due to fast hand friction which dries up the lube. The conventional condom does not give the right sensation with hand massage and is much more suitable when thrusting up some hot constricting pussy. I have tried placing a magazine on a music stand, thus leaving both hands free, but the snag is that I feel stupid being so deliberate, and can't get it up!

* * *

Having been a Nexus reader for quite a few years, hope you don't mind if I write to thank you. I am a dedicated wanker and have yet to find another provides me with so many fantastic orgasms. This may be a new one for your records, but my total hang-up is sex words. Reading your stories, full of words like 'cunt', 'spunk', 'shag' and 'fuck' can raise it to its six-inch limit. The fuckable females with pony-racing tack and suckable cunts set my cock and balls on the way to orgasm. The fact is, I do have women, but even after a good fuck I still enjoy an old-fashioned one off the wrist, with no one but myself to please.

I don't need a shrink to tell me how I became latched on to dirty words and a compulsive tosser. When I was about sixteen I accidentally found a sex magazine. I almost passed out when my eyes caught those words in print. 'He fucked her steadily, her cunt tight and velvety, his hard, long prick shafting in and out, almost bursting to release his viscous spunk.' Although I was used to playing with my well-developed cock, that night I had a mind-blowing wank and shot what felt like my largest ever load of come. Since then I have been a dirty word fanatic and connected them with a satisfying wank and a relaxing draining of the balls.

A Glossary of Terms

Curious: *adj*; person has an unfulfilled sexual interest in their own gender

Dogging: *n*; voyeuristic, exhibitionistic or group sex activity often carried out in known local lovers' lanes or beauty spots

Fornophilia: *n*; a type of bondage; arousal by the idea or practice of turning people into furniture

Gerontophilia: *n*; sexual attraction to the elderly and to the physical features of old age

Masochist: *n*; one who finds arousal in receiving pain – may or may not be a submissive

Romantic Love: *n, phrase*; a widespread and powerful fixation which originated, as we now understand it, with twelfth-century courtly poetry, and which is similar to what William Burroughs calls 'recognition'. I did receive a few replies that referred to it.

Submissive: *n, adj*; one who finds arousal in loss of control, and potentially in feelings of shame/humiliation/embarrassment – may or may not be a masochist

Switch: *n*; one who finds pleasure in dominant *and* submissive behaviour

Wife-watcher: *n*; one who enjoys watching their own partner engage in sexual activity with others

Nexus

Male Sexual Fantasy in the 21st Century

A. QUESTIONS ABOUT YOU

1. What is your age? . . . years

2. Are you single . . . or in a long-term partnership or marriage . . .?

3. Are you: heterosexual . . . homosexual . . . or bisexual . . .?

What, if anything, do you find offensive? Please list things – objects, actions or even attitudes – which are to do with sex or which are often associated with sex and which offend you.

4. in photographs, on television or in films

5. in novels

6. in real life

```
┌─────────────────────────────────────────┐
│                                         │
│                                         │
│                                         │
│                                         │
└─────────────────────────────────────────┘
```

Please fill in as much information in the following section as you wish. If you prefer to remain anonymous, that's fine.

7. Name _____

8. Address _____

_____

_____

9. phone number if you wish _____

10. your occupation _____

B. ABOUT YOUR SEXUAL FANTASIES (Definition: What you think about when you think about sex in such a way that you become sexually aroused.)

1. How often, on average, do you have sexual fantasies: several times a day? ... Once a day? ... A few times a week? ... A few times a month? ... Hardly ever? ...

2. Do your fantasies tend to have recurring themes or subjects? ... Or is each fantasy very different? ...

3. If there are recurring themes or subjects, what are they?

4. Do you have a current favourite fantasy, or a fantasy that you enjoy more than most? Please write your fantasy – from the very beginning – in the space below. If you want to go into a lot of detail – and I'd like you to – please continue on separate sheets of paper.

C. ABOUT YOUR SEXUALITY

1. Think back to when you were discovering your sexuality, your sexual orientation, and the sexual themes that are now part of your personality. What did you find erotic in those days? What things (for instance films, or books, or items of clothing) or people or experiences were a turn-on?

2. What things or people or experiences are particular turn-ons now?

3. Describe – in detail, don't be shy – the best sex you've ever had (so far!). As before, continue on a separate sheet if you prefer.

4. What would improve your sex life?

```
┌─────────────────────────────────────────┐
│                                         │
│                                         │
│                                         │
│                                         │
└─────────────────────────────────────────┘
```

D. WHAT NEXT

First of all, please feel free to write as much as you like. The purpose of this questionnaire is to gather written material for possible inclusion in a book to be published by the Nexus imprint. Replies returned to Nexus on or with this questionnaire become the copyright of Nexus and may freely be reproduced by Nexus. Nexus undertakes not to publish, nor reveal to anyone other than persons employed by Virgin Books Ltd, the names, addresses, telephone numbers or email addresses of any person who returns this questionnaire.

Finally, send your completed questionnaire, along with anything else you've written or anything else you'd like to send to help me understand your erotic imagination, to this address:

Paul Scott
Nexus
FREEPOST
LON 3566
W6 9HA

Or email it to: *paulscott01uk@yahoo.co.uk*

Remember, it's Freepost, so if you're sending it from within the UK you don't need to use a stamp.

NEXUS NEW BOOKS

SATURNALIA
An Anthology of Bizarre Erotica
Edited by Paul Scott

Saturnalia features the most exciting, surreal and sadomasochistic extracts from a selection of classic masterpieces concerning sex and sexuality. From de Sade and Sacher-Masoch to Beardsley, Huysmans, Octave Mirbeau and many others, along with confections as diverse as Swinburne and Li Yu.

Saturnalia gathers together prose that straddles the divide between erotic and literary fiction, and strips away the hidebound to give you a flavour of some of the most robust, fetishistic works ever written. Books which are a treat for anyone who likes to think about sex for themselves, and writing that has lost none of its power to thrill, excite and shock.

Saturnalia was published in June 2002, and *Saturnalia II* is provisionally due to be published in April 2003.

ISBN: 0 352 33717 6   £7.99

LESBIAN SEX SECRETS FOR MEN

The Ultimate Guide to Pleasing and Satisfying a Woman – from Women who Know
Jamie Goddard and Kurt Brungardt

Lesbian Sex Secrets for Men opens the bedroom door of gay women to answer your most intimate questions about making love to the woman you love. From the titillating to the taboo, from kisses to climaxes, from G-spots to the Big O, here is the ultimate road map to the hot spots and nether regions of the female body that will help you create new levels of intimacy and sexual pleasure.

Let *Lesbian Sex Secrets for Men* help you discover:
● What women really want in bed
● How to master the Sapphic arts – and enjoy the female body in an entirely new way
● The pleasures of sensual massage
● The ins and outs of erotic love – total surrender and total control
● Your most important sexual tool (a hint – it's between your ears)
● Ways of opening up the channels of sexual communication
● Where fantasies come in
● The joy of toys
● Relationship roadblocks, and how to get past them
Plus: tips, techniques and sex games

Filled with interviews, surveys and the uncensored voices of women speaking honestly about what they want in a lover, *Lesbian Sex Secrets for Men* is more than a manual of gymnastic sexual techniques – it's the ultimate guide to satisfying a woman's sexual needs and desires.

7 November 2002   ISBN: 0 352 33724 9

NEXUS BACKLIST

This information is correct at time of printing. For up-to-date information, please visit our website at www.nexus-books.co.uk

All books are priced at £5.99 unless another price is given.

Nexus books with a contemporary setting

ACCIDENTS WILL HAPPEN	Lucy Golden ISBN 0 352 33596 3	☐
ANGEL	Lindsay Gordon ISBN 0 352 33590 4	☐
BARE BEHIND £6.99	Penny Birch ISBN 0 352 33721 4	☐
BEAST	Wendy Swanscombe ISBN 0 352 33649 8	☐
THE BLACK FLAME	Lisette Ashton ISBN 0 352 33668 4	☐
BROUGHT TO HEEL	Arabella Knight ISBN 0 352 33508 4	☐
CAGED!	Yolanda Celbridge ISBN 0 352 33650 1	☐
CANDY IN CAPTIVITY	Arabella Knight ISBN 0 352 33495 9	☐
CAPTIVES OF THE PRIVATE HOUSE	Esme Ombreux ISBN 0 352 33619 6	☐
CHERI CHASTISED £6.99	Yolanda Celbridge ISBN 0 352 33707 9	☐
DANCE OF SUBMISSION	Lisette Ashton ISBN 0 352 33450 9	☐
DIRTY LAUNDRY £6.99	Penny Birch ISBN 0 352 33680 3	☐
DISCIPLINED SKIN	Wendy Swanscombe ISBN 0 352 33541 6	☐

THE TORTURE CHAMBER	Lisette Ashton	☐
	ISBN 0 352 33530 0	
UNIFORM DOLL	Penny Birch	☐
£6.99	ISBN 0 352 33698 6	
WHIP HAND	G. C. Scott	☐
£6.99	ISBN 0 352 33694 3	
THE YOUNG WIFE	Stephanie Calvin	☐
	ISBN 0 352 33502 5	

Nexus books with Ancient and Fantasy settings

CAPTIVE	Aishling Morgan	☐
	ISBN 0 352 33585 8	
DEEP BLUE	Aishling Morgan	☐
	ISBN 0 352 33600 5	
DUNGEONS OF LIDIR	Aran Ashe	☐
	ISBN 0 352 33506 8	
INNOCENT	Aishling Morgan	☐
£6.99	ISBN 0 352 33699 4	
MAIDEN	Aishling Morgan	☐
	ISBN 0 352 33466 5	
NYMPHS OF DIONYSUS	Susan Tinoff	☐
£4.99	ISBN 0 352 33150 X	
PLEASURE TOY	Aishling Morgan	☐
	ISBN 0 352 33634 X	
SLAVE MINES OF TORMUNIL	Aran Ashe	☐
£6.99	ISBN 0 352 33695 1	
THE SLAVE OF LIDIR	Aran Ashe	☐
	ISBN 0 352 33504 1	
TIGER, TIGER	Aishling Morgan	☐
	ISBN 0 352 33455 X	

Period

CONFESSION OF AN ENGLISH SLAVE	Yolanda Celbridge	☐
	ISBN 0 352 33433 9	
THE MASTER OF CASTLELEIGH	Jacqueline Bellevois	☐
	ISBN 0 352 32644 7	
PURITY	Aishling Morgan	☐
	ISBN 0 352 33510 6	
VELVET SKIN	Aishling Morgan	☐
	ISBN 0 352 33660 9	

Samplers and collections

NEW EROTICA 5	Various ISBN 0 352 33540 8	☐
EROTICON 1	Various ISBN 0 352 33593 9	☐
EROTICON 2	Various ISBN 0 352 33594 7	☐
EROTICON 3	Various ISBN 0 352 33597 1	☐
EROTICON 4	Various ISBN 0 352 33602 1	☐
THE NEXUS LETTERS	Various ISBN 0 352 33621 8	☐
SATURNALIA £7.99	ed. Paul Scott ISBN 0 352 33717 6	☐
MY SECRET GARDEN SHED £7.99	ed. Paul Scott ISBN 0 352 33725 7	☐

Nexus Classics

A new imprint dedicated to putting the finest works of erotic fiction back in print.

AMANDA IN THE PRIVATE HOUSE £6.99	Esme Ombreux ISBN 0 352 33705 2	☐
BAD PENNY	Penny Birch ISBN 0 352 33661 7	☐
BRAT £6.99	Penny Birch ISBN 0 352 33674 9	☐
DARK DELIGHTS £6.99	Maria del Rey ISBN 0 352 33667 6	☐
DARK DESIRES	Maria del Rey ISBN 0 352 33648 X	☐
DISPLAYS OF INNOCENTS £6.99	Lucy Golden ISBN 0 352 33679 X	☐
DISCIPLINE OF THE PRIVATE HOUSE £6.99	Esme Ombreux ISBN 0 352 33459 2	☐
EDEN UNVEILED	Maria del Rey ISBN 0 352 33542 4	☐

- - - - - ✂ -

Please send me the books I have ticked above.

Name   ....

Address   ....

                ....

                ....

                .... Post code....................

Send to: **Cash Sales, Nexus Books, Thames Wharf Studios, Rainville Road, London W6 9HA**

US customers: for prices and details of how to order books for delivery by mail, call 1-800-343-4499.

Please enclose a cheque or postal order, made payable to **Nexus Books Ltd**, to the value of the books you have ordered plus postage and packing costs as follows:

   UK and BFPO – £1.00 for the first book, 50p for each subsequent book.

   Overseas (including Republic of Ireland) – £2.00 for the first book, £1.00 for each subsequent book.

If you would prefer to pay by VISA, ACCESS/MASTERCARD, AMEX, DINERS CLUB or SWITCH, please write your card number and expiry date here:

....

Please allow up to 28 days for delivery.

Signature ....

Our privacy policy.

We will not disclose information you supply us to any other parties. We will not disclose any information which identifies you personally to any person without your express consent.

From time to time we may send out information about Nexus books and special offers. Please tick here if you do *not* wish to receive Nexus information. ☐

- - - - - ✂ -